LINES AROUND THE CITY

'Our Modern Travelling Facilities' from 'The Baillie' of 16 December 1896
suggested that the new Subway was too much to cope with . . .

LINES AROUND THE CITY

David Harvie

LINDSAY
PUBLICATIONS

First published 1997 by
Lindsay Publications, Glasgow

For Gavin and Isabelle

ISBN 1 898169 11 X

British Library Cataloguing-in-Publication Data
A Catalogue record for this book is available from
the British Library

Designed and typeset by Janet Watson and
Mitchell Graphics, Glasgow

Cover: 'Buchanan Street 1902'
Watercolour by Horatio Thomson (1885–1903)
courtesy of Hunterian Art Gallery, University of Glasgow

Printed and bound in Great Britain by Redwood Books

CONTENTS

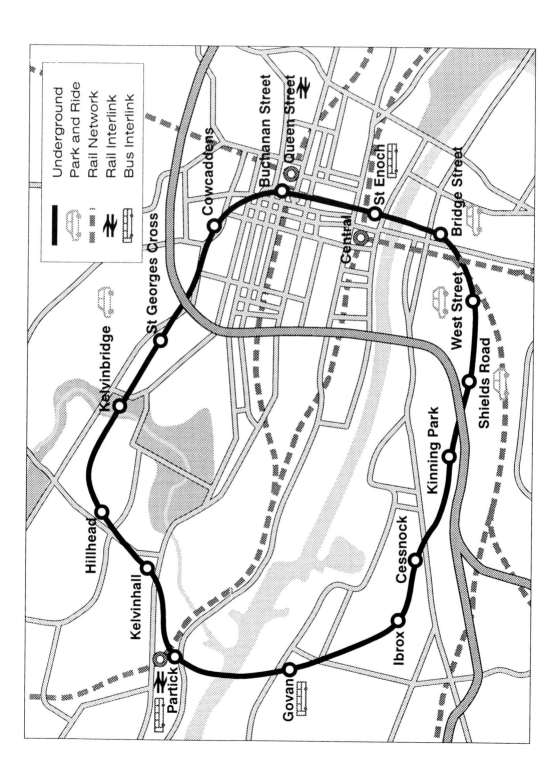

PREFACE

THIS BOOK has been inspired by two distinct influences. One is a long-term curiosity in the notion that there is a powerful 'sense of place' which exists everywhere but which may be more potent in places which are subject to constant change — cities, in particular. The idea that places may appear to be both changed yet familiar, that they somehow convey resonances from an unfamiliar past, is neither impractical or mystical. It is no more than the result of the commonplace interaction of people with each other and with the landscape in which they have lived their lives.

Having accepted that the idea may be interesting, it is an easy step to conclude that an effective way to consider it further is through the words of people who have taken the trouble to attempt to describe the places in question. Such descriptions need not always have been intended as systematically accurate, or even truthful. Scientific accuracy is not all. The contribution of fiction could not so conveniently be denied. Many of the fictional extracts in this anthology contain, in my view, the most illuminating, dynamic and sensitive descriptions of Glasgow.

The second inspiration is another book. In 1994, Dorothy Meade and Tatiana Wolff published *Lines on The Underground*, an anthology based on the London Underground, having spent almost half a century since their student days gathering material. Quite apart from the pleasure of reading their volume, there is something attractive about the conjunction of The Subterranean and the descriptively rich passages on the page.

This present volume, then, is happily predicated on the centenary in December 1996 (or, possibly, January 1997!) of the Glasgow District Subway. Comparison with the London Underground is, of course, unhelpful, and likewise there are considerable differences between this volume and that of Meade and Wolff. Over 350 stations offer an opportunity perhaps for only one extract each. With as few as fifteen Glasgow stations to visit, a wider selection of material is possible. Fiction, poetry, journalism, personal memoirs and trade directories are among the variety of sources employed. I have also added a degree of narrative commentary, which I hope will assist in linking the extracts and explaining the context. While the main feature must be the text, I hope that occasional photographs, drawings and other illustrations will add to rather than distract from the potency of the writing.

I have to confess in a few instances to modest cheating, in that a passage which an author may have set in one part of the city has been transported to provide a description of another. One example is an extract which clearly belongs in the Gorbals, but which is used in Hillhead as a sympathetic cross-reference to the author's description of the aspirations of families to move to the better areas. I think I have been sensitive in this regard and, in any case, make it clear on those few occasions when I have resorted to this course.

Sometimes, authors themselves make matters confusing. A J Cronin, for example, whose descriptions of Glasgow are undeniably good, invents new names and re-invents geography from time to time, making it difficult to be precisely certain of his setting. Alternatively, it makes it easier for an anthologist to impose his own interpretation.

On other occasions, an author provides a wonderful 'back reference'. Archie Hind's hero Mat in *The Dear Green Place* finds himself in a brilliantly contemplative wander by the River Clyde, recalling the visit to the same place almost two hundred years earlier by James Boswell.

This anthology is essentially a personal selection which is meant to stir the memory and refresh images of Glasgow. It will be no secondary effect if readers are lured into reading books which they might not otherwise pursue. Better still, books might be re-read which have been forgotten. And no shame is attached to the discovery of favourite passages.

Some of the books which appear here in extract have been out of print for many years. This should not deter those within reach of Glasgow's splendid Mitchell Library, where archival collections of newspapers and journals are as available as most of the other sources represented here. Some titles have been reprinted in recent years, most notably in the Canongate Classics series. Local libraries can also arrange inter-library loans of a surprising amount of material. An excellent starting-point is *The Glasgow Novel, a Survey and Bibliography*, by Moira Burgess, which can be purchased in Glasgow Libraries.

I hope that this book brings pleasure and some surprise to all its readers. Even better if, as you turn its pages, you happen to be plunging under the Clyde aboard Glasgow's much-loved Clockwork Orange!

David Harvie

INTRODUCTION

IT IS not the purpose of this volume to dwell at length on the history and technicalities of the Glasgow Underground — no doubt in its centenary year others will fulfil that object with distinction. However, the purposes of this anthology will be served by a brief description of the system which began its life as the Glasgow District Subway and despite various changes over the years, during which its title has officially been changed to Underground, still retains the affectionate and popular name of The Subway.

To all intents and purposes it was, and remains, a small-scale railway — a toy train set to some visitors. A circular route of six and a half miles has twin tunnels serving fifteen stations, with the circles running services in opposite directions. The small bore of the tunnels necessitated narrow-gauge tracks of 4' 00'' rather than standard gauge, and consequent small, short trains and platforms. Although there have been a number of proposals for the extension of the system over the years, the fact of its non-standard dimensions has been a significant element in the failure of such schemes.

When the first plan for a Subway was made in 1887, Glasgow was a busy city with an intense need for improved public transport, a situation exacerbated by a shortage of river crossings. Railways already operating in the city centre included the Glasgow City & District Railway, which ran steam trains on an underground link through Queen Street and Charing Cross between the sections of the North British Railway which lay to the east and west of the city centre. That success goaded the rival Caledonian Railway to promote its Glasgow Central Railway, running on a parallel underground route to that of the NBR.

The privately promoted Glasgow District Subway was to run on the north of the river only, from St. Enoch Square to Partick, using an entirely underground route, but it failed to win the necessary support in parliament. An extended scheme was proposed the following year, with a circular route which crossed the river twice. This was opposed by the Clyde Navigation Trust, which anticipated interference with its own schemes for improvements to the river navigation. However, following the adoption of a plan to build the pedestrian and vehicle tunnel at Finnieston, the climate became more favourable to a railway tunnel under the Clyde. In 1890, a parliamentary Bill was promoted for the Subway system which exists today. This had the support of the independent Burghs of Partick, Govan and Kinning Park, as well as of Glasgow University Senate and the city Trades' Council. The Bill was successful, and construction began in March 1891.

The most notable characteristic of the new underground was that it was cable-hauled. The first scheme was to have had the trains permanently fixed to a cable running between the tracks. Stations were to be 700 yards apart, with trains attached to the cable at 1,400 yard intervals. The seemingly bizarre plan was that all trains would stop, start and travel between stations simultaneously, constantly under the whim of the cable. The system as eventually built was still cable-hauled but the cable was free running, at a height of about two inches above the track, and trains were fitted with gripper mechanisms, therefore allowing independent traction.

A power station was built at Scotland Street, on the South Side. Two 2,000 horse-power steam engines, powered by coal, were used to drive the two 57-ton wire rope cables (one for each circle) at a constant speed of about 13 miles per hour.

The engines were fitted with 50-ton flywheels to help modulate the variable load and the cables were fed over a system of pulleys and drums before and after entering a 'tension run' which helped absorb fluctuating loads and allowed regular maintenance.

Each cable was an endless loop which travelled around its own circle via the power house and tension run. Of necessity, there had to be one splice in each cable, but one which had to be the same diameter as the standard cable in order not to foul the gripper mechanism on the trains. The splices could be up to ninety feet in length, and were painted white to assist gripmen in avoiding the cable at that point. Some station-masters developed the habit of chalking on the ends of the platforms the times when the splices last passed through the station, as a guide to gripmen.

Stations were arranged so that platforms sat at the highest point on a gradient. A train would release the cable some distance short of a platform and use the approaching up-gradient to aid its smooth stop at the far end of the platform. On starting off, it would coast for a short distance on the down-gradient before gripping the cable. These techniques ensured that stopping and starting were relatively smooth, and that excessive strain was not placed on either the cables or the tension mechanism. One potential problem of 'snatching' was that the cable could leap several feet from its guides between the running rails, with no certainty that it would return to its proper position, or that it could easily be re-positioned without considerable disruption.

The cable system proved to be remarkably reliable and it demonstrated at least one surprising advantage — it was easily able to function during occasional flooding incidents. During one episode following a burst water main, trains kept running until the water came over the floor-boards of the carriages. It has been claimed on more than one occasion that the Glasgow Subway was the only underground railway in the world to have its own rowing-boat. Certainly, on one occasion in 1954, during a rainstorm, a boat was hurriedly borrowed from Hogganfield Loch and pushed off into the tunnel at Govan to investigate an innundation.

The future seemed bright for the new railway. However, by 1901, the Glasgow Corporation Tramways had been completely electrified, and the new quick, clean and cheap trams somewhat put the gloomy Subway to shame. There was even a strange crisis of legal identity at one point. A dispute arose over whether or not the system was a 'railway' within the meaning of the appropriate legislation. Consequently, in 1914 a new parliamentary Act was passed formally legalising the Glasgow District Subway Railway Company.

The system paid its way, modestly, until the First War when rising costs became a problem. The post-war depression, with consequent declining traffic, made matters almost terminal. Protracted negotiations to sell the system began with Glasgow Corporation. Discussions did not proceed very well and at one point it was announced that the system would be permanently closed. Eventually, however, the Corporation bought the Subway in 1922 for the bargain price of £385,000, representing only 5% of the original capital investment. The system subsequently became part of the Corporation Transport Department.

After a few years under Corporation ownership, trials were undertaken with a view to complete electrification of the system, and the change-over to electrified traction was completed in 1935. The modernisation seems to have been a bit half-hearted, undertaken at a total cost of £94,000 as against the 1922 estimate of one million pounds. Electric power was easily supplied from existing tramway supply stations and where possible, equipment was retained and recycled, with the original carriage electric lighting system supplied from rails running along the tunnel walls and old track being used as electric conductors. Incidentally, the electric lighting for carriages was a progressive original feature, installed in preference to the dangerous use of gas or paraffin. The newly re-christened 'Underground' tried to project a bright new image, but it was substantially the old system dressed-up slightly. The stations, for example, were still the same dingy, smelly dungeons of old, their entrances often situated in ill-lit alley-ways, or seemingly disguised in what were tenement buildings or shops.

However, there was soon a proposal to extend the system. In 1937, a plan was discussed to build a line from Robroyston in the north-east, through Buchanan Street and Bridge Street, and out to Newlands and King's Park in the south-east. This scheme was dashed by the Second War, which might also have been expected to strangle the Subway's prospects in much the same way as the First War had done. However, wartime regulations affected the ability of trams, buses and surface railways to use adequate lighting during the hours of darkness, so the Subway became especially popular during the war.

In the late 1940s came a further proposal for extending the system. This would have constructed a further complete circular route to the east of the city centre. Built to standard dimensions, the new circle could not have been physically grafted onto the original Subway, but there were three interchange stations planned, at Bridge Street, St Enoch and Buchanan Street. Further stations were proposed at Kennedy Street (Parliamentary Road), Blochairn, Dinart Street, Carntyne, Rigby Street, Belvedere Hospital (London Road), Dalmarnock, Richmond Park and Hutcheson Square (Caledonia Road). There was considerable public support for the extension, but costs were declared to be prohibitive and the scheme was shelved.

When the system was closed in 1976 for modernisation, it was renowned for possessing the oldest original railway rolling stock still in use. Travellers at the time will testify to the 'character' of the system, which was without doubt a monument to its original builders and to the generations of maintenance engineers who modified, cannibalised and employed great ingenuity to keep the eighty-year-old trains running. When Strathclyde Passenger Transport Executive opened the totally refurbished system in 1980, with new rolling stock and rebuilt stations, there was a wave of nostalgia for what had been lost. The famous 'shoogle' was largely gone, although some of it remains thanks to the original changing gradients and curves. The new orange-liveried stock was immediately nicknamed the 'Clockwork Orange'.

What people seemed to miss most was the smell! There are enthusiasts who claimed that there had indeed been a characteristic smell lingering from the days of cable operation, when Archangel Tar had been used to protect and lubricate the cables.

No doubt, in time, nostalgia will build for the present system, which can be confident of the same popularity and position in the affections of Glaswegians as was the 1896 vintage. And despite setbacks to proposals for a new tramway system, the transport pulse of the city will no doubt remain a-flutter.

Railway stations — and by extension, underground stations — have always given particular streets and districts of any city a special *cachet* and often allowed names to survive the predatory advances of planners and developers.

In some small way, what this anthology hopes to achieve is to celebrate the sense of place which is often contributed to by railway stations and certainly conveyed by the memoirs of diarists and the invention of novelists.

(ACKNOWLEDGEMENTS)

AMONGST many others, I am grateful to Brian Osborne and Louis Stott for comments and suggestions; to members of staff of the Glasgow Room and Mr Hamish Whyte and staff of the Arts Dept of the Mitchell Library, Glasgow; to the Glasgow City Archives; to Winnie Tyrrell of Glasgow Museums Photographic Library; to Michael Schmidt and Carcanet Press; and to Dr David Sutton of the Writers and their Copyright Holders Project at Reading University.

The editor and publisher gratefully acknowledge permission to reproduce extracts from the following copyright material in this book:

Old Glasgow Club Transactions, courtesy of Mrs Mary McKinlay and the committee of the Old Glasgow Club.

The Clyde River and Firth (1907); E*rchie & Jimmy Swan; Para Handy Tales* and *The Brave Days* (1931), Neil Munro, courtesy of Mrs Lesley Bratton.

The Breadmakers, © Copyright Margaret Thomson Davis 1972. Currently available from B & W Publishing: courtesy of Margaret Thomson Davis.

The Yairds, John F Fergus, first published 1924 and in 'Noise and Smoky Breath' (1983) courtesy of Mrs Helen Evers.

Scottish Journey, Edwin Muir, first published 1935, courtesy of Mainstream Publishing.

Tinsel, courtesy of Alan Spence, first published in *Its Colours arc Fine* by Collins in 1977 and reprinted by Phoenix Paperbacks in 1997.

Glasgow 1960, Hugh MacDiarmid, first published 1935 and in 'Noise and Smoky Breath' (1983) courtesy of Carcanet Press.

The Shipbuilders, George Blake, first published 1935 and by B & W Publishing, reprinted by permission of David Higham Associates.

Glasgow Stations, Colin Johnston and John R Hume, 1979, courtesy of David & Charles.

The Glasgow Herald, courtesy of Caledonian Publishing Ltd.

Unlikely Stories, Mostly, Alasdair Gray, 1983, courtesy of Alasdair Gray and Canongate Publishing.

The Last Grain Race, Eric Newby, Secker & Warburg, 1956, courtesy of Eric Newby.

Glasgow, Iain Crichton Smith, published in 1969 and in 'Noise and Smoky Breath' (1983), courtesy of Carcanet Press.

Glasgow's Smiles, Farquhar McLay, published 1988, courtesy of Farquhar McLay.

Brond, Frederic Lindsay, published 1983, courtesy of Frederic Lindsay.

Dance of the Apprentices, Edward Gaitens, first published 1948, courtesy of Canongate Publishing.

The Jeely Piece Song, Adam McNaughtan, published 1967 and in 'Noise and Smoky Breath' (1983), courtesy of Adam McNaughtan.

A Song of Sixpence, A J Cronin, first published by Heinemann in 1964, courtesy of Mr Vincent Cronin.

Wax Fruit, © Copyright Guy McCrone, first published by Constable in 1947, courtesy of Guy McCrone and A M Heath.

Mungo, George Woden, first published 1932, Hutchinson.

Poor Tom, Edwin Muir, first published 1932, J M Dent, courtesy of Orion Publishing.

No Mean City, Alexander McArthur and H Kingsley Long, first published 1935 and by Transworld Publishers Ltd, courtesy of The C W Daniel Co. Ltd.

Swing Hammer Swing!, Jeff Torrington, first published by Secker & Warburg, 1992, courtesy of Reed Books.

The Maggie, Ealing Studios, screenplay by William Rose, courtesy of UGC (UK).

Shannon's Way, A J Cronin, first published in 1948, courtesy of Victor Gollancz, publishers, and Mr Vincent Cronin.

A Regional History of the Railways of Great Britain, Volume Six, Scotland, The Lowlands and The Borders, John Thomas, published by David & Charles, 1971, courtesy of Atlantic Transport Publishers.

The Railway Station, A Social History, Jeffrey Richards and John M MacKenzie, 1986, by permission of Oxford University Press.

Among You Taking Notes, The Wartime Diary of Naomi Mitchison, 1939–45, Naomi Mitchison, edited by Dorothy Sheridan, published 1985, courtesy of Victor Gollancz, publishers.

The Dear Green Place, Archie Hind, published 1966, courtesy of Archie Hind.

The Busconductor Hines, James Kelman, published 1984, courtesy of Polygon, publishers.

Laidlaw, first published 1977 and *The Papers of Tony Veitch* (1983), William McIlvanney, courtesy of Hodder & Stoughton, publishers.

Wild Geese Overhead, Neil Gunn, first published 1939, and 1991, courtesy of Chambers Harrap Publishers Ltd.

Open The Door, Catherine Carswell, first published in 1920 (and to be reprinted by Canongate), courtesy of John Carswell.

The Hert O The City, Duncan Glen, published 1976 and in 'Noise and Smoky Breath' (1983), courtesy of Duncan Glen.

At Central Station, Edwin Morgan, first published in Akros 1978 and in 'Noise and Smoky Breath' (1983), courtesy of Carcanet Press.

Mince Collop Close, George Blake, published 1923, Grant Richards, reprinted by permission of David Higham Associates.

Lanark, Alasdair Gray, first published 1981, courtesy of Alasdair Gray and Canongate Publishing.

1982 Janine, Alasdair Gray, courtesy of Alasdair Gray and Random House, publishers.

Glasgow Sonnets, Edwin Morgan, first published 1972 and in 'Noise and Smoky Breath' (1983), courtesy of Carcanet Press.

Somewhere between St. George's Cross and Hillhead Underground, Jack Withers, published 1988, courtesy of Jack Withers.

The Trial of Madeleine Smith, in the 'Notable British Trials Series, edited by F Tennyson Jesse, published 1927, courtesy of Joan Colenbrander.

The quotation from *Mr Alfred MA*, George Friel, published in 1972, is reproduced by permission of The Calder Educational Trust, London.

Before Dark, Stewart Conn, reprinted by permission of Bloodaxe Books Ltd, from 'In The Kibble Palace' by Stewart Conn (Bloodaxe Books, 1987).

By Kelvin Water, Tom McGrath, published in Lines Review 1972 and in 'Noise and Smoky Breath' (1983), courtesy of Tom McGrath.

Pride of Lions, Geddes Thomson, published by Chapman and in 'Streets of Stone (1985), courtesy of Geddes Thomson.

A Sense of Order, Stewart Conn, reprinted by permission of Bloodaxe Books Ltd, from 'In The Kibble Palace' by Stewart Conn (Bloodaxe Books, 1987).

Growing up in The Gorbals, Ralph Glasser, published by Chatto & Windus, 1986, courtesy of David Higham Associates.

Obituary, Liz Lochhead, from 'Dreaming Frankenstein and Collected Poems' 1984 and 'Noise and Smoky Breath' (1983), courtesy of Polygon, publishers.

Major Operation, James Barke, published in 1936 and 1970, Chivers, courtesy of David Higham Associates.

School Friend, Bill McCorkindale, first published by Caithness Books 1975, and in 'Noise and Smoky Breath' (1983) courtesy of Louise McCorkindale.

Scotland The Brave, Iain Hamilton, courtesy of Mrs Jean Hamilton.

GOVAN CROSS

IBROX
CESSNOCK
KINNING PARK
SHIELDS ROAD
WEST STREET
BRIDGE STREET
ST ENOCH
BUCHANAN STREET
COWCADDENS
ST GEORGE'S CROSS
KELVINBRIDGE
HILLHEAD
KELVIN HALL
PARTICK

For: Bus Interchange: Elder Park and Library; Pearce Institute

WHILE GOVAN is the location of many important technical and support facilities, St Enoch is often thought of as the headquarters of the Subway system. However, for the purposes of this anthology we shall make a start at Govan Cross Station at 6 Greenhaugh Street, for no other reason than that the first train set off at an unearthly hour on its maiden journey from this station a century ago.

On the opening day, 25,000 people travelled on the new Subway, bringing in, at a one penny fare, a total of £104.

> The first train yesterday left Govan Cross at 5 o'clock in the morning running by way of Partick, a second leaving Copland Road and running by way of Kinning Park. The early cars were largely taken advantage of by work-men, and from eight to ten o'clock there was a great rush of all classes, the various outlying stations especially being fairly besieged.
>
> from *The Glasgow Herald* Tuesday 15 December 1896

In earlier days, Govan was a distinctive village, and in its later existence as part of Glasgow it continued to retain an independence which is still recognisable today. Some of that independent spirit can be found in the following descriptive passages.

> The lands of Govan are generally well enclosed and divided; and a considerable proportion of those on the S. side of the river is farmed by the proprietors themselves. With the industry and activity of the farmers, which

are nowhere more conspicuous, several other circumstances have evidently occurred, in bringing this parish to its present state of improvement. Its vicinity to Glasgow, which, till lately, has for a number of years been increasing with astonishing rapidity, procures a sure and ready market for its produce, and furnishes a most convenient and plentiful supply of the best manure; and as no less than four branches of the King's highway run through the parish, the carriage to Glasgow of the articles it produces, and of the manure brought from thence, particularly on the S. side of the Clyde, is attended with no sort of difficulty.

from *The Statistical Account* vol. xiv, 1798

Govan was at one time described as a *'gret and ane large village upon the water of Clyd.'* It was further referred to as a *'picturesquely situated village and that there could not be anything prettier than the scene of which the little village of Govan was the centre.'* Coast landladies are not a new thing for, in these days, houses were offered to let for holidays and people from Glasgow, which was then on the north side of the Clyde only, came to the sandy shores of Govan to spend their summer holidays. It was mentioned that the water at Govan at that time was clear and clean, and was frequently used for the making of the inhabitants' tea. Here and there, green fields extended to the water's edge, and of an evening many of the village families could be seen spending their leisure moments on these fields. The hub of village life was in the Water Row, and there, in the Ferry Bot Inn, visitors and natives would assemble to spend an hour, probably too convivial at times. Until within recent years, the house formerly named the Ferry Bot Inn still stood. There, about 1804, The White

Glasgow City Archives

Greenhaugh Street, Govan, 1932. The Subway station, still with its cast-iron canopy, seems to leap out from a row of tenement shopfronts

Wine Club of Glasgow held its monthly meeting, but it has been suggested that the wine was not so white as the name would seem to indicate.

from *Old Glasgow Club Transactions:* 'Some aspects of old Govan'
Walter McIndoe, 11 November 1937

And some fictional 'proof' of holidays in Govan...

I got through wi' the measles real easy: but the chincough set doon unco sair on my system – in truth, I got sic a shake, and croichled awa' sae lang, that my mither had to tak' me doon to the waterside at Govan for a change o' air, where we bidet for three weeks wi' my mither's marriet sister, Mrs. Brodie, and where we baith experienced great benefit to oor health frae the change o' scene and the caller air.

from *Martha Spreull,* Zachary Fleming (Henry Johnston)
Being chapters in the life of a single wumman, 1884

When Neil Munro – the creator of Para Handy, of whom more later – described Govan in 1907, his tone was rather dismissive:

Govan, but for the possession of a Provost of its own, and a different design of lamp-posts, is virtually as much a part of Glasgow as Bermondsey is of London; there is no breach in the continuity of noisy, high-walled and thickly populated streets that lead to it from the city's heart; nothing survives of the rural character it had in the 1830s when the gourmets of Glasgow – with cautious circumlocution for fear of the elders, you may be sure – used to walk there for its famous Sunday salmon suppers which gave it a local fame as great as Greenwich has earned by its white-bait.

The Mitchell Library

Main Street, Govan in 1872, complete with thatched roofs, in the days when folk went there on holiday

Except for the reckless and ill-fated fish I have already referred to as venturing at long intervals up to the docks, the only salmon to come to Govan nowadays arrives in cans from British Columbia, but there are men alive who recollect the fishery which existed here long after nets were drawn for the last time on green banks where now are the wharves of Glasgow.

from *The Clyde, River and Firth*, Neil Munro, 1907

But fiction still annointed Govan with character:

The Old Govan Fair was always held on the first Friday in June and dated back to the fifteenth century, when Govan itself was barely a village and Clydend had no existence at all.

It had been originally granted by ecclesiastical rescript and at one time was the occasion of annual festival and holiday when the local deacon was elected.

The village band turned out to play for the retiring deacon at his residence, and it was also the custom for the band to halt at each public house en route in order to serenade the landlord. He, in return, was expected to come out into the street with a bottle of 'the cratur' with which he regaled all the bandsmen. The result was that although the music had been distinct and lively at the beginning of the march it deteriorated into a mere confusion of hiccoughing sounds long before the journey ended. The main function, however, was not to pay court to the retiring deacon but to elect a new one. After the solemn business of the election was over, the proceedings quickly gave way to jovial rejoicings. A procession formed and marched to the boundaries of the village carrying the famous 'sheep's head' hoisted aloft on a pole and gaily decorated. The sheep's head with its shaggy hair and big curling horns had always been the emblem of the Burgh. Legend had it that, long ago before ships were built in Govan, a pretty girl had come to serve in the manse and a young man had begun to court her and eventually asked for her hand. The cleric put his veto on the alliance and refused the youth permission to continue seeing the girl. The young man nevertheless succeeded in carrying her off and, in celebration, or revenge, he cut off the heads of the sheep in the glebe lands of the manse and left these grim relics lying on the ground. The villagers, siding with the young couple, took the choicest specimen of the sheeps' heads and did it honour publicly by carrying it on the Fair Day all along the village street to the ancient 'Ferrie Bot' hostel at Water Row, where they all got 'roarin' fou and unco' happy' drinking the health of the happy couple.

The traditional sheep's head was still carried but the procession had grown with the place. Govan had at one time been a village on the banks of the River Clyde, but over the years increasing industrialisation exploded the once-peaceful water's edge with the endless clamour of the shipyards and the giant cranes crowding to reach the sky. Now, there were high honeycombs of

The Mitchell Library, (Graham Collection)

Waverley Inn, Water Row, Govan in 1861 ('The Ferrie Bot Inn')

tenement buildings behind the yards. Bustling shops with fruit and vegetables spilling out on to the pavements, draperies with dense doorways of hangers bulging with clothes. Dark brown, sawdust-floored pubs at every corner where money could be spent when men were working. When they were not, gloomy, dusty caverns of pawn shops with brass balls above where precious possessions might fetch a few shillings.

The Breadmakers, Margaret Thomson Davis, 1972

No anthology which includes Govan could ignore the area's main occupation – and preoccupation. . .

No better illustration of the development of steam navigation and marine construction during the last half century can be given than the rise and progress of the firm of Messrs Alexander Stephen & Sons (now one of the largest and most important ship-builders in the United Kingdom).

Although the Stephen family have been shipbuilders for over a century (originally belonged to Aberdeen) it was not until 1851 that the firm, fully alive to the fact that the Clyde had become the leading river for marine architecture, removed the seat of their operations to Kelvinhaugh.

In 1870 their rapidly growing requirements necessitated a further extension of premises, and the firm acquired by purchase the fine old estate of Linthouse. This property gives a frontage to the river of 1,070 feet, and allows full accommodation for eleven ships. It covers an area of some 32 acres, which is now occupied by the works and the handsome range of workmen's dwellings erected by the firm. The property extends 1,400 feet from the river to the Govan Road, from which the firm have a broad-gauge railway running down to the ship-building department and intersecting the engineering and boiler shops.

In the handsomely appointed private offices of the firm, into which we were first ushered when recently making a tour of inspection of the establishment, are three hundred or so of the most beautiful and exquisitely finished models it has ever been our good fortune to examine. Mr Alexander Stephen takes great pride in the elaborate pieces of workmanship, and pardonably boasts that he himself has had a hand in the building of each one, the formation of the model of every vessel the firm puts into the water being completed in a technical studio which was originally used as a billiard room.

from *Strattens' Glasgow and its Environs*, 1891

THE YAIRDS

I've wrocht amang them, man and boy, for mair nor fifty year,
I canna bear to quit them yet noo that I'm auld an' sere,
The Yairds is just the life o' me, the music's in my bluid
O' hammers striking strong an true on rivets loweing rid;
I'm auld, I ken, but, Goad be thank'd! I hivna lost my pride
In honest wark on bonny boats that's built upon the Clyde.

Frae Broomielaw to Kempoch Point I ken them every yin,
I kent them when I wis a wean when I could hardly rin;
I kent them as a rivet boy, I kent them in my prime,
An' tho' there's been an unco wheen o' chainges in my time,
Yet still it's aye a bonny sicht to see them in their pride,
Wi' 'weys' laid doun an' some big boat a' ready for the tide.

It's graun' to see the boats grow up frae keel to upper strake,
An' ken it's a' guid honest wark an' no' an unce o' fake;
It's graun to see the muckle frames staun' up like leafless trees,
To hear the clang o' plates an' see the rivet furnace bleeze,
To see the bonny boats tak' shape just like a leevin' thing,
Eh, man, but it's a bonny sicht an' fit to please a king.

I've helped to build a wheen o' them in mony a different yaird,
Frae barges up to battleships the Empire for to guaird,
An' eh, the names I could reca' o' men noo passed awa
Wha planned and built the boats lang syne, aye trig and strang and braw.
The men hae gane, but left ahint a legacy o' fame,
For honest wark an' bonny boats that gied the Clyde its name.

Tod an' McGregor, Napier tae, John Elder, an' the Scott's,
Wi' auld Wull Fyfe, awa' doun bye, aye buildin' bonny yachts,
The 'Limited,' an' Simonses, the Tamson's at Clydebank
(That's noo John Broon's), an' Stephens whaur the puir *Daphne* sank,
An' Caird's, an' Connel's, Barclay Curles, an' Russell, an' Dunlop,
An' Fairfield, Beardmore's, Tammy Seath's – I've wrocht in every shop.

Ye'll hear it said the 'Black Squad' drink an' break their time forbye,
Weel I jaloose we hae oor fauts – jist let the jaw gang by;
But this I'll say that, gin we drink an' break oor time as weel,
Wi' a' oor fauts, by Goad! we ken jist hoo to lay a keel,
An' build a boat that nane can beat in a' the warld beside,
The best o' wark, the bonniest boats aye come frae oot the Clyde.

John F Fergus, 1924

APPALLING DISASTER ON THE CLYDE
VESSEL CAPSIZES AT A LAUNCH: GREAT LOSS OF LIFE

The River Clyde was yesterday the scene of a terrible disaster involving a lamentable loss of life. A small vessel, the *Daphne*, of about 500 tons, was being launched from the yard of Messrs Stephens & Sons, Govan, when just as she entered the water, she heeled over and sank almost immediately.

from *The Glasgow Herald* 4 July, 1883

The People's Palace

The Daphne *sunk off Stephens' yard, 3 July 1883*

146 men and boys who were completing work on *Daphne*'s interior were drowned. It was three weeks before the ship could be raised and the bodies recovered. However, unlike expected responses to similar incidents today, the official government inquiry heard its first witnesses only seven days after the accident and the Report was submitted to the Home Secretary Sir William Vernon Harcourt the following month.

> We have now seen that the *Daphne* had very small initial stability in the launching condition; that this was attended, very unexpectedly to all concerned, by the absence of the usual power of rapidly acquiring stability as she inclined; that the smallness of the initial stability was in part due to the presence on the bridge-deck, poop, and forecastle of very heavy equipments, and the consequent raising of the centre of gravity; that there were many loose materials of considerable weight on board, and also many workpeople, by the shifting of some of which a new demand was made upon the stability when the ship inclined considerably; and to these facts may be added the further one that the engines (but not the boilers) were secured on board when the launch took place.
>
> The lives lost by the capsizing of the *Daphne* will not have been lost in vain if they arouse shipowners and shipbuilders generally to the fact that the stability of their ships is a subject which deserves vastly more consideration than it at present receives.
>
> from Sir Edward Reed's Report to the Home Secretary, August 1883

No one was found to be culpable, nor was there any suggestion that any of the large number of workers on board during the launch were there as the result of any compulsion by the builders. The Report's demand was simply for 'substantial improvement upon the present arrangements'.

> In a city in which the shipping and shipbuilding interests are of such paramount importance, it will readily be conceded that the business of the compass adjuster, binnacle constructor, and general nautical instrument maker is one the importance and value of which cannot easily be over-estimated nor surpassed. Foremost, both in respect of antiquity of establishment and magnitude of business connection, among the many Scotch houses similarly engaged must be ranked the well-known firm of Messrs Whyte, Thomson and Co, of Broomielaw, Glasgow, and Neptune Works, Harmony Row, Govan.
>
> The works at Govan are admirably equipped with all the most approved appliances, plant and machinery, and every facility is afforded for the rapid and expeditious execution of all work engaged in. The firm here manufacture such items as cabin and engine-room lamps, steam pressure gauges, steam vacuum gauges, compound steam gauges, engine counters, engine indicators, lamps of all kinds, and cabin fittings of various descriptions, and everything is made from the raw material. The firm are chronometer makers to the

Admiralty, and also fits out the Cunard Line, Donald Currie & Co, British India, Orient, Royal Mail Steam Packet Co, Union Steamship Co of New Zealand, the Donaldson Line, etc, etc.

from Strattens' Glasgow and its Environs, 1891

Travelling through depression-struck Lanarkshire in 1933, the poet and critic Edwin Muir resolved to make a journey through Scotland, and to record 'the state of the nation'. In holding up his diagnostic mirror to the face of Scotland, he brought a dreadful reality to many unseeing eyes. He was scathing of the conditions in which many of his compatriots lived.

The slums in a Scottish industrial town are generally to be found either near the factories or in the oldest and most dilapidated of the tenements. Glasgow has slums of both kinds. There are certain factories which produce such a stench that to live near them involves a loss of self-respect, and the surrounding houses in such cases turn into slums. Many such factories are scattered over the South Side. On the other hand the tenements near the shipyards have mostly a clean and orderly look; and one can still feel (though they have degenerated a great deal since shipbuilding virtually stopped) that the people who lived in them led for many years a self-respecting existence and had a tradition. And immediately behind some of the shipyards one may come upon green fields dotted with trees.

from Scottish Journey, Edwin Muir, 1935

The Mitchell Library

Govan Horse Ferry

23

The staccato stutter of the Benlin riveters filled to bursting point the whole Main Road and Dessie Street and all the streets in Clydend with a fiendish metallic noise that echoed all over Glasgow, even drowning the rumble and clanging of the tramcars.

The people in Dessie Street had learned to live with it, to ignore it, to adapt their outside voices to broad, lusty bawls accentuated by elastic mouths that looked as if they were trying to make lip-reading as easy as possible for deaf folk.

Women leaned out of windows and shouted pleasantries to each other and exchanged titbits of gossip. Little girls in the dusty street below squealed and giggled and teetered and tripped about in their mothers' high-heeled shoes and too-long dresses and held on to huge-brimmed, feather-trimmed hats. Others were lost in rapt concentration, their eyes glued to a fast bouncing ball.

from *The Breadmakers*, Margaret Thomson Davis, 1972

GOVAN CROSS

IBROX

CESSNOCK
KINNING PARK
SHIELDS ROAD
WEST STREET
BRIDGE STREET
ST ENOCH
BUCHANAN STREET
COWCADDENS
ST GEORGE'S CROSS
KELVINBRIDGE
HILLHEAD
KELVIN HALL
PARTICK

For: Ibrox Stadium; Govan Town Hall; Bellahouston Park

THIS STATION – for many, the most important – was originally planned to be at nearby Brighton Street. It opened as Copland Road Station, at No 140 Copland Road and it was burdened with that name until the system was modernised and the station's name was changed to admit its real purpose in life.

> Ibrox is both British and Gaelic and is said to mean the haunt of the badger (brock, Gaelic *Bruic*). Another possibility is from a rentaller – there are two names in the registers, Broc and Brokas. In a charter of 1580 the name is given as Ibrokes.
>
> from *The origin and history of Glasgow streets*, Hugh Macintosh, 1902

Mr James Swan has lived for fifteen years in Ibrox. For the first six months he thought it horrible, and ever since he has vexed himself to think how foolish he was not to have gone there sooner. That is life. Men are like pot plants. You shift a geranium into a new pot, and for weeks it wilts disconsolate, till some fine sunny day it seems to realise that other geraniums seem happy enough in the same sort of pots, and that it isn't the pot that matters really. Whereupon the geranium (which is actually a pelargonium) strikes fresh roots into the soil, spreads out a broader leaf, throws out a couple of blossoms, and delights in making the best of it. It takes the first prize at the local flower show; content is the best fertiliser. Jimmy Swan, after fifteen years at Ibrox, thinks Ibrox is the centre of the solar system. Take him to Langside or

Partickhill, and he feels chilly; at Dennistoun he feels himself a foreigner, and looks at passing tramcars for the Southside as an exile from Scotland, haunting the quays of Melbourne, looks at ships from the Clyde with the names of Denny or Fairfield on their brasses. Jimmy said to me the other day, 'I canna think how people can live ony where else than Ibrox. It's the best place in the world.' 'How?' I asked. 'Well,' said he, 'it's-it's-it's-it's Ibrox!'

from 'Linoleum' – *Erchie & Jimmy Swan*, Neil Munro, 1917

From the lobby he heard the toilet being flushed so he waited in the dark until he heard the slam of the toilet door then the flop of Mrs. Dolan's feet on the stairs. The Dolans lived in the single end, the middle door of the three on their landing. The third house, another room and kitchen, was empty for the moment because the Andersons had emigrated to Canada.

When he heard Mrs Dolan closing the door he stepped out on to the landing and slid down the bannister to the stairhead. In the toilet there was only one small window very high up, and he left the door slightly open to let light seep in from the stairhead.

A pigeon landed on the window-ledge and sat there gurgling and hooing, its feathers ruffled up into a ball. To pull the plug he climbed up on to the seat and swung on the chain, squawking out a Tarzan-call. The pigeon flurried off, scared by the noise, and he dropped from his creeperchain, six inches to the floor.

He looked out through the stairhead window. Late afternoon. Out across the back and a patch of wasteground, over factory roofs and across a railway line stood Ibrox Stadium. He could see a patch of terracing and the roof of the stand. The pressbox on top looked like a little castle. When Rangers were playing at home you could count the goals and near misses just by listening to the roars. Today there was only a reserve game and the noise could hardly be heard. Soon it would be dark and they'd have to put on the floodlights.

from *Tinsel*, Alan Spence, 1977

Football, of course, is the great Glasgow obsession, but thankfully, it is possible, with wit, to poke some gentle fun. . . maybe not from within the crowd, however. . .

GLASGOW, 1960

Returning to Glasgow after long exile
Nothing seemed to me to have changed its style.
Buses and trams all labelled 'To Ibrox'
Swung past packed tight as they'd hold with folks.
Football match, I concluded, but just to make sure
I asked; and the man looked at me fell dour,

Then said, 'Where in God's name are *you* frae, sir?
It'll be a record gate, but the cause o' the stir
Is a debate on 'la loi de l'effort converti'
Between Professor MacFadyen and a Spainish pairty.'
I gasped. The newsboys came running along,
'Special! Turkish Poet's Abstruse New Song.
Scottish Authors' Opinions' – and, holy snakes,
I saw the edition sell like hot cakes!

Hugh MacDiarmid, 1935

Fiction, capable of celebrating the place, also sometimes manages to reflect a hint of the pernicious bigotry:

When, five minutes before time, the men from the East were awarded a penalty kick, Danny's heart stopped beating for a space, and when the fouled forward sent the ball flying foolishly over the net, it nearly burst. The Rangers would win. 'Stick it, lads!' he yelled again and again. 'Kick the tripes out the dirty Papists!' The Rangers would win. They must win. . . A spirt of whistle; and, by God, they had won!

In immediate, swift reaction, Danny turned then and, without a word to his neighbours, started to fight his way to the top of the terracing and along the fence that crowned it to the stairs and the open gate. To the feelings of those he jostled and pushed he gave not the slightest thought. Now the battle was for a place in the Subway, and he ran as soon as he could, hurtling down the road, into the odorous maw of Copland Road station and through the closing door of a train that had already started on its journey northwards.

He even got a seat and was glad of it. Now he felt tired and flat after that long stand on a step of beaten cinders and nearly two hours of extremely emotional strain. It had been a hell of an afternoon, right enough!

At Partick Cross he paused only to buy an evening paper before darting into the public-house nearest at hand. It was disappointing that the barman already knew the result, thanks to the daily miracle of the Press, and he saw in a glance at the stop-press that his coupon was burst again – Queen's Park down to St Mirren at home, the bunch of stiffs!

from *The Shipbuilders*, George Blake, 1935

The Subway's 'odorous maw' was very much one of the characteristic features which inevitably signalled either closure or renaissance. Thankfully, the latter prevailed – but not until the 1970s. Even before the re-opening in 1980, a kind of nostalgia broke out:

'The Subway' was so much a part of Glasgow life that it is difficult to believe that it has gone. Gone not to dereliction and decay, but to be reincarnated in a modern form, with all the much-talked-about features like interchange stations with British Rail, escalators, and rather less of the familiar 'shoogle' of the cars on the undulating track. The old is never the same as the new, and it seems appropriate to include some of the city's more obscure stations in a book devoted largely to the grand and impressive. Where but in Glasgow could you apparently enter a railway station through a retail draper's establishment, or be assailed by the aroma of kippering fish in the centre of a city? Several of the stations on the Underground were conveniently situated next door to licensed premises, while Copland Road station was specially adapted to handle the crowds for Glasgow Rangers football club's celebrated Ibrox Stadium.

from *Glasgow Stations*, Colin Johnston and John R Hume, 1979

Ibrox Park had seen a disaster at the Scotland–England International in 1902, when terracing collapsed and twenty-three fans were killed. History was sadly to repeat itself.

On Saturday, 2 January 1971, the annual 'Old Firm' match at Ibrox between Rangers and Celtic resulted in a draw 1-1. As in Blake's fiction, a late incident (in this case Rangers' equaliser) caused many in the crowd to turn and head for the top of the terracing, at Stairway 13, while those who had left moments earlier tried to make their way back.

The outcome was catastrophic. Crush barriers collapsed and, in the chaos that followed, sixty-six fans were crushed to death.

Re-assessments of the evidence twenty-five years later have come no closer to identifying the causes than did the original inquiry.

An enquiry to be held into the disaster at Ibrox Stadium on Saturday in which 66 persons died and 145 were injured, could have world-wide repercussions.

Mr Edward Heath, the Prime Minister, will today receive a personal report from Mr Gordon Campbell, Secretary of State for Scotland, who is flying to London to tell ministers of what he learned during his visit yesterday to Glasgow.

from *The Glasgow Herald* Monday 4 January, 1971

The resulting enquiry could find no definitive cause for the tragedy, which has remained as a painful stain on Glasgow's collective sporting memory.

GOVAN CROSS
IBROX

CESSNOCK

KINNING PARK
SHIELDS ROAD
WEST STREET
BRIDGE STREET
ST ENOCH
BUCHANAN STREET
COWCADDENS
ST GEORGE'S CROSS
KELVINBRIDGE
HILLHEAD
KELVIN HALL
PARTICK

For: Bellahouston Park

CESSNOCK IS the least celebrated of all the areas penetrated by the Subway. Long before the system was thought of, the district was distinctly rural and undeveloped. In the 1870s, individual officers of the Clyde Navigation Trust began secretly buying small parcels of land belonging to the estates of Cessnock, Middleton, Bankton and Haughead, which lay to the east of Govan and south of Plantation Quay. When they sold their holdings collectively to the Trust and plans were announced in 1882 for a huge dock complex, there was a public outcry. The fuss was not about the proposed development of what became Princes Dock, but about the alteration to existing roads.

When the Subway was built, the station was originally to be known as Walmer Crescent, but with its address at No 1A Cessnock Street, its official name was sealed.

In 1988 the dock area became famous as the site of the Glasgow Garden Festival, since when it has lain substantially derelict, although at the time of writing there are murmurings of a large 'multi-media centre' for the site.

Luckily, Alasdair Gray has given us an unlikely story of Cessnock:

Nowadays Cessnock is a heavily built-upon part of industrial Glasgow, but two hundred and seventy-three years ago you would have seen something very different. You would have seen a swamp with a duck-pond in the middle and a few wretched hovels round the edge. The inmates of these hovels earned a living by knitting caps and mufflers for the inhabitants of Glasgow who, even then, wore almost nothing else. The money got from this back-breaking industry was pitifully inadequate. Old Cessnock was neither beautiful nor healthy. The old folk living there were too old or twisted by rheumatism to move out. Yet this dismal and uninteresting hamlet saw the beginning of that movement which historians call The Industrial Revolution; for here, in seventeen hundred and seven, was born Vague McMenamy, inventor of the crankshaft which made the Revolution possible.

from 'The Crank that Made the Revolution' in *Unlikely Stories, Mostly,* Alasdair Gray, 1951

The next extract belongs, strictly speaking, directly across the river at Queen's Dock. However, it is included here since it has a flavour of the city docks, and in any case, it conveys an authentic resonance.

We passed the night of the 26th at anchor off the Tail of the Bank. I still had hay fever.

'Soon cure that,' said the Captain. 'Down in the chain-locker.'

As the cable came in over the windlass and straight down into the vertical locker deep in the ship I coiled it down link by link. The bottom of the Clyde at Tail of the Bank was very muddy.

At last on the 27th of June we were warped with infinite difficulty into Queen's Dock.

'Coming again?' asked the Captain some days later, after some good parties, as he inked in my discharge as Ordinary Seaman and handed over some fragments of pay. 'Make a man of you next time.'

'I'll think it over,' I answered.

The Vuitton trunk was loaded onto a taxi. Suddenly those of the crew still on board seemed remote and once more strangers.

'I'll write to you,' said Kroner. 'We'll try to get to the Grand Banks.' It was a project we had discussed all through the homeward voyage. Now it seemed absurd.

'Central Station,' I said to the taxi-driver. He was even more villainous-looking than the one in Belfast.

'You'll be glad to get out of that bitch,' he said, jerking a thumb over his shoulder.

'You think so, do you,' I said.

'I do.'

'Then you don't know what you're talking about.'

Now we were turning through the dock gates into the main road where the trams rattled and swayed. I looked back at *Moshulu* whose masts and yards towered above the sheds in the June sunshine.

I never saw her again.

from *The Last Grain Race*, Eric Newby, 1972

The following poem laments the passing of the dock areas of the South Side – Cessnock, Plantation, Mavisbank and Govan itself. Following the decline in shipbuilding, these areas were changed utterly by a series of Comprehensive Development Area designations in the 1970s.

GLASGOW

City, cauldron of a shapeless fire,
bubbling with brash Irish and a future

that stares from fifteen stories towards the Clyde.
The cotton and tobacco plants have died

Plantation St is withered. You love your ships,
hate your police, in whisky-coloured sleeps

adore your footballers. Victoria's not amused
at Celtic Park or Ibrox where the horsed

dice-capped policemen, seared by pure flame
trot in white gauntlets round your serious game

and the roaring furnaces bank your last pride.
They shed the rotting tenements flying goalward.

Iain Crichton Smith, 1969

GOVAN CROSS
IBROX
CESSNOCK

KINNING PARK

SHIELDS ROAD
WEST STREET
BRIDGE STREET
ST ENOCH
BUCHANAN STREET
COWCADDENS
ST GEORGE'S CROSS
KELVINBRIDGE
HILLHEAD
KELVIN HALL
PARTICK

For: Kinning Park

THE BURGH of Kinning Park was formed on the lands of the estate of the same name. Kinning House itself stood until about 1870 to the east of Kinning Place on Paisley Road.

The name derivation is from *cunyie* or *cunnyng*, meaning a corner. On some old maps, Cunnyng Park is shown as a field in an angle formed by the intersection of a burn and the road.

Kinning Park Station was probably originally to have been called either Plantation or Cornwall Street (being situated at No. 82 Cornwall Street). The tunnels in the vicinity are at the least depth of all the system, being only about seven feet below ground.

The first extract superbly conveys the atmosphere of the dense, industrialised district which Kinning Park had become during the last century. It was written by a visiting London journalist, who had come to visit one of the flourishing industries:

> The day in question was typically Glaswegian: dull and murky overhead, with fresh air at a premium, and smoke *ad libitum*; plenty of honest Glasgow mud, semi-plastic with recent moisture underfoot – a day hardly calculated to induce the exercise of superfluous energy. But these things trouble not the hardy Scotch west-countryman, and suburban Glasgow – which is industrial Glasgow – was as busy, as noisy, and as active in a thousand and one different ways as ever it was – only seemingly more so. Such I found to be the case as I made my way to the Kinning Park region of that ever-extending city. There is

no Park now, though I suppose there once was; but that is only a detail which the Glasgow people have no time to consider. Now it is all business at Kinning Park.

Ironworks, engineering shops, and quite an *olla podrida* of industrial establishments of all sorts and conditions find there a congenial home; and if, from an aesthetic point of view, the change may not be pleasing to the eye, it means wealth and material prosperity; and the citizens of Glasgow, being essentially practical, or nothing, regard this metamorphosis of recent years rather favourably.

from *The Mining Journal* 14 September 1889

The Mitchell Library

Part of the olla podrida *of Kinning Park industry*

Although the name Gorbals strictly belonged to those parts of Laurieston and Hutchesontown which adjoined the Clyde, there was also a wider use of that colourful name:

Gorbals, which lies E of Govan along the S bank of the Clyde, is the largest and most populous district in the city, and is indeed large enough of itself to rival Aberdeen or Dundee. It might in every way be described as the Southwark of Glasgow. It measures about 2 miles by 1 mile, and has, in connection with new manufactures, with railway works, and with harbour works, spread rapidly and widely between 1835 and the present time. It comprises the districts of Plantation, Kinning Park, Kingston, Tradeston, Laurieston, and Hutchesontown. Some idea of the rapid growth of these districts may be gathered from the fact that, between 1861 and 1871, the population of Kinning Park increased from 651 to 7,217, and between 1871 and 1891 again to 13,679.

from *Groome's Ordnance Gazetteer, 1893-95*

The next poem angrily condemns the planners who, for reasons good and bad, swept away so much of Glasgow in the 1960s. Probably the main complaint is not so much what they did, but the manner in which it was all done. Much of that part of Kinning Park described above has been covered in swathes of concrete motorway.

GLASGOW'S SMILES

Dear Sir, I must advise you that
Your house is going to be knocked flat

We're going to take you from your slum
And put you in the lovely Drum

Or Easterhouse or some other scheme
Where the rain falls hard and the wind blows keen

Your little street is lean and scrawny,
The ringroad's legs are big and brawny

And it squelches as it goes –
The only question being, Whose toes?

All must fall to let it pass,
Kinnen Park, Anderston, Port Dundas.

Your meagre little street won't shine
When leviathan calls to dine.

When leviathan comes on wheels
He's sure to be set on bigger meals.

We hope you won't quarrel with what we're doing
And kick up all that hullaballooing;

The Gorbals and Cowcaddens went
Withoot a murmur of dissent.

But if you must, then, say your say:
You may petition us all day.

And if wiseacres say, What a futile lark!
Just point to the toilet in the park.

That heap of rubble by the gate
Was a public pissoir till of late,

And when you mounted your campaign
Did we regard it with disdain?

Bulldozers at a single blow
Lewd and libidinous laid low,

And certain folks were most astonished
To find their rendezvous demolished.

True, that was part of another plan,
An 'unattended toilets' ban

And purely a police decision
Before we saw your nice petition:

(A confidential memo, that,
Which some fool couldn't keep under his hat,

But what's democracy about
If you can't come clean when the secret's out?)

Nevertheless the cooncil's dream,
Auld Glesca guttit oot an clean

Wull make some rich and ithers famous
An segregate thae yins thit shame us.

(This hamcly daub we thocht tae scryveit
Fur fear yer lugs were sairly deaveit

No tae say yer puir wee harnes
Wi' Inglis bureaucratic terms,

As weel's tae show, jist like in law
Scots can ootbureaucrat them aa

an tho we clack an tho we glower
We're great idolators o power.

Fur thae puir sowls thit urnae followin:
WE'RE GONNIE KICK THIS CITIE'S HOLE IN!)

There's glory and there's hygiene too
When you put your toes in leviathan's stew:

Think if in time to come they'll say,
He moved his arse for the motorway!

Or, Nero got it right in one –
A town smells better when it's gone.

Farquhar McLay, 1988

The last extract, properly belonging in Govan, where its author set it, is used here simply for the flavour which it brings – a flavour which belonged in many areas of the city familiar to the Subway user, at least in its early days.

He thought the crowd lounging at the corner looked familiar and, sure enough, as he got nearer he saw it was Slasher Dawson and some of his gang. Slasher was well known and feared in the district. Lil Fowler made good use of him as a muscle-man. Her extortionate rates of interest were seldom questioned when Slasher was called in to collect. Slasher had more razor scars on his face and neck than any man in Glasgow. He couldn't be much older than Jimmy but his Frankenstein stitch-puckered face and his giant humped-up shoulders made it difficult to guess his age, and nobody wanted to. Nobody wanted to do anything to Slasher Dawson or say anything about Slasher Dawson, much to many a Glasgow policeman's chagrin.

His gang in comparison were unhealthy, undersized mice, nervous fleshless ferrets as much afraid of him as anyone else but under the continual strain of trying to keep up with his crime and violence in order to please him. They had no idea of any other way to survive, living as they did around the other corner in Dixon Street where Slasher also had his abode.

from *The Breadmakers*, Margaret Thomson Davis, 1972

GOVAN CROSS
IBROX
CESSNOCK
KINNING PARK
SHIELDS ROAD
WEST STREET
BRIDGE STREET
ST ENOCH
BUCHANAN STREET
COWCADDENS
ST GEORGE'S CROSS
KELVINBRIDGE
HILLHEAD
KELVIN HALL
PARTICK

For: Scotland Street School Museum

SHIELDS ROAD station, at No 368 Scotland Street, lies at the edge of the Kinning Park area and the hotch-potch of multifarious industry was very much a feature between Scotland Street and the river.

Shields Road was one of those parts of Glasgow, nicely noted below, in which the grime and noise of the industrial city lived cheek by jowl with the handsome face of substantial rich living.

In the early days, when the Subway was operated by cable, the Cable Power House was situated in Scotland Street, not far from the station. Here, two huge steam engines drove the cables over a massive flywheel weighing 50 tons and with a diameter of 25 feet.

A valuable and long-standing repute attaches to the business of Messrs John McFarlane & Co who are the oldest representatives of the sailmaking trade in Glasgow. The firm's fine new building in Shields Road is acknowledged one of the most completely organised concerns of the kind in the Western Metropolis.

They consign largely to China, Calcutta, Bombay, Columbia, New Zealand and the Colonies, and also nearly all the Continental ports and all the seaports of the United Kingdom, and derive a large share of the prosperity of their business from the vitality and always increasing success of their export trade. Messrs McFarlane's sails have been always readily identified by the sound and sterling quality of the canvas employed in their manufacture, and in both sails and tents they embody such reputed fabrics as are known to emanate from the canvas manufacturing houses of Gourock and Arbroath.

from an advertisement in *Strattens' Glasgow and its Environs*, 1891

The following extracts illustrate that feature of Shields Road which allowed the workshops of the Empire to exist as neighbours of the once-grand (and mostly still-grand) mansions of Pollokshields.

In Glasgow you can drive out of a slum street into one beside it that looks like an Adam terrace in Edinburgh. It is a city of contrasts. The house Brond stopped the car at was handsome. It was like the house some friends lived in; five students in a ground floor flat; they ate in a room that had a carved wood mantelpiece thirteen feet high. It was the kind of house the merchants and the shipping barons built for themselves when the city was rich. Now in my friends' flat holes like woodworm in the mantelpiece showed where the lads played darts after they had been drinking.

from *Brond*, Frederic Lindsay, 1983

Pollokshields is a pleasant suburb, composed principally of detached villas, with one or two terraces, lying about two miles south-west from the Royal Exchange. The houses are substantially built, and the streets are spacious and well planned. From the facilities with which it can be reached from the city, it is a favourite residence with many business men. The best routes are by the Shawlands cars, which pass near it on the east, in addition to which omnibuses run to and from Glasgow several times a day; or by train either from St Enoch to Strathbungo and Pollokshields Stations, or from the Central to Shields Road.

from *Kirkwood's Dictionary of Glasgow*, 1884

'Where do you live, Norman?' he asked.
    'Glasgow,' Norman replied.
    'Quite so. And what part? Let us get to the details.'
    'Resthaven.'
    'Well, what street is it in?'
    'It's not a street. It's a drive.
    At that he sagged so badly that Danny decided he must keep moving. So, with linked arms, away they went. Shields Road Norman identified because of the whistling of trains and a great puff of steam on each side of the road. By the time they reached the top of the hill where the flats of Pollokshields ended and the dotted houses began with names upon the gateposts, Dan was fairly tired. There it was that Nairn remembered his chief amusement of the evening. He leant against a garden wall and hiccuped.
    Dan was disgusted. He dreaded that his charge was to be of the crapulous kind. But no, this was hilarity, not sickness. Norman was convulsed with merriment.

'But I canna put that on the bills!' he whooped, and had to stand still to laugh.

'Come on, come on,' said Dan. 'Straighten up. Here's a polisman. Do you want to be run in?'

from *The Staff at Simsons*, Frederick Niven, 1937

The Mitchell Library

Shields Road industry, advertised in the 1888 Exhibition Catalogue

GOVAN CROSS
IBROX
CESSNOCK
KINNING PARK
SHIELDS ROAD

WEST STREET

BRIDGE STREET
ST ENOCH
BUCHANAN STREET
COWCADDENS
ST GEORGE'S CROSS
KELVINBRIDGE
HILLHEAD
KELVIN HALL
PARTICK

WEST STREET station, situated at No 299 West Street, was originally to have been called Tradeston, the district of which West Street forms the western boundary. That part of Glasgow, along with Kingston, Gorbals, Laurieston and Hutchesontown became a harsh, neglected crucible in which the large population lived amongst the factories, machine-shops and warehouses that were the Victorian city's lifeblood.

For most of last century, a private railway ran down the middle of the street, substantially destroying the neighbourhood. It was owned and operated by William Dixon, proprietor of a colliery at Govan, who used the line to transport coal from pit to harbour, and then on to his glass-works at Dumbarton.

Glasgow Mercury, 1 May, 1792
'The Provost-Haugh, about 24 acres, has been purchased at private sale for no less than four thousand pounds. This added to the other pleasure ground along the river belonging to the city, is a valuable acquisition. The philanthropic Mr Howard, when surveying this tract of ground, declared it to be of inestimable value for preserving the health of the inhabitants.

An acre of ground down the river, where the Coal Key stood, and bounded by the Kinning House burn, was sold by public roup for £350 sterling. It was let for £5 yearly for sixteen years past.'

I remember the Coal Quay, which stood at the present ferry, west end of Windmillcroft. It was built by the Dumbarton Glassworks Company to convey coals from the lands of Little Govan to their works at Dumbarton.

The river was then deeper at the Coal Quay than at the Broomielaw. There was a timber tramway from the Little Govan coal works to the said Quay, which ran through the lands of Kingston, and by the road on the east side of Springfield. I have walked upon this tramroad, which I believe was the first of our Glasgow railways. The Dumbarton Glassworks Company also possessed a tramroad on the north side of the Clyde, from the coal works in the neighbourhood of Gartnavel; but I do not recollect the exact place in the river where the coals were shipped.

The footpath along the south bank of the river from the bridge westward, crossed the south end of the Coal Quay, and when the traveller came to the Kinning House burn, he was obliged to find his way over it by a narrow wooden plank, without any protective railing. At this time there was a small wood on the lands of Windmillcroft, within a hedge on the south of the footpath which ran along the banks of the river. This wood stood nearly on the place now occupied as the north extremity of West Street.

from *Glasgow and its Environs*, 'Senex' (Robert Reid), 1884

There is at present a great deal of discussion as to the best method of providing more thorough cross-river communication further west than the Broomielaw Bridge. The systems proposed include swing and high-level bridges, tunnels, and increased ferry accommodation, but up till now no actual step has been taken. In the meantime all communication is conducted by a number of small ferry steamers, provided by the Clyde Trustees, connecting the following points:

NORTH SIDE	*SOUTH SIDE*
York Street	West Street
Clyde Street	Entrance to Kingston Dock
Hydepark Street	Foot of Springfield Quay
Finnieston Street	Mavisbank Quay
Kelvinhaugh Street	Maxwell Street, Govan
Partick Wharf	Water Row, Govan

from *Kirkwood's Dictionary of Glasgow*, 1884

The next extract portrays a strong sense of a vibrant life '. . . seethin' on the dunghill o' Capitalism'. The modern proliferation of traffic in the streets has made the following scene unlikely today:

Two distinct games of football were being played in this last portion of the street with about forty rough lads and youths wildly shouting as they kicked about an immense football made of paper and string. Knots of ragged children, crowding the pavement, played old Scottish singing games, dancing, clapping hands; boys whipped peeries, played jorries or ran madly with steel cleek and gird; with a rusty, rattling bike, some boys were learning

The Herald

The latter days of the Whiteinch passenger ferry in 1963 still evoked an earlier period

to cycle; girls hopped under skipping ropes, played peever or tossed coloured chukkies; two boys on roller-skates sailed recklessly along the smooth macadam; the pavements were crudely chalked with juvenile games; from top storeys downward at every other window husbands and wives leant out on cushions or pillows, groups of youths or girls stood at the closes, old people sat there on stools and from first storey windows tenants shouted conversation with neighbours at the close.

'This is life with the lid off,' said Eddy as they crossed the street, threading among the rushing footballers.

'It's the Mob at play, the slaves o' ceevilisation seethin' on the dunghill o' Capitalism,' said Donald, relishing his phrases which he believed he had just invented.

They regarded the 'Mob' with tragic superiority, then suddenly laughed heartily as a little bowlegged goalkeeper in a desperate dash at the ball, tripped headlong over one of the goalposts, a pile of heaped jackets and caps.

'It must be hard fur wee Rabbie tae save the ba' wi' they bandy legs o' his,' said Donald. 'Ye could run a tramway through them!'

from *Dance of the Apprentices*, Edward Gaitens, 1948

The references to rickets and 'windae-hingers' will no doubt provoke memories of the period, such as the ubiquitous 'jeely piece', which flew from the later (multi-) storeys.

THE JEELY PIECE SONG

I'm a skyscraper wean; I live on the nineteenth flair,
But I'm no' gaun oot tae play ony mair,
'Cause since we moved tae Castlemilk, I'm wastin' away
'Cause I'm gettin' wan meal less every day:

Chorus: *Oh ye cannae fling pieces oot a twenty storey flat,*
Seven hundred hungry weans'll testify to that.
If it's butter, cheese, or jeely, if the breid is plain or pan,
The odds against it reaching earth are ninety-nine tae wan.

On the first day ma maw flung oot a daud o' Hovis broon;
It came skytin' oot the windae and went up insteid o' doon.
Noo every twenty-seven hoors it comes back intae sight
'Cause ma piece went intae orbit and became a satellite.

On the second day ma maw flung me a piece oot wance again.
It went and hut the pilot in a fast low-flying plane.
He scraped it aff his goggles, shouting through the intercom,
'The Clydeside Reds huv goat me wi' a breid-an-jeely bomb.'

On the third day ma maw thought she would try another throw.
The Salvation Army Band was staunin' doon below.
'Onward, Christian Soldiers' was the piece they should've played
But the oompah man was playing a piece an' marmalade.

We've wrote away to Oxfam to try an' get some aid,
An' a' the weans in Castlemilk have formed a 'piece brigade.'
We're gonnae march to George's Square demanding civil rights
Like nae mair hooses ower piece-flinging height.

Adam McNaughtan, 1967

Considering that the firm of Blacklock and MacArthur was only established about fourteen years ago, the importance which the Clydesdale Paint, Oil and Colour Works owned by them have, during that period, attained is most gratifying. Situated in Dale Street, with the offices and warehouses adjoining in West Street, Tradeston, the works contain grinding rooms, colour floors, tank rooms containing oil tanks, cask stores, etc.

Their oil colours include various kinds of whites, blues, reds and browns, blacks, greens, yellows, and liquid paints ready mixed; anti-fouling compositions, anti-corrosion paint in all colours, colours in turpentine and water, tinted paints and dryers. Of dry colours they make blacks, blues, browns, greens, lakes, ochres, pinks, reds, whites and yellows. Oils, turpentines, varnishes, etc., they trade in also, while under the head of sundries is a formidable list of chemicals, of requisites for painters, gilders, builders, engineers, cabinet makers, and other tradesmen.

from an advertisement in *Strattens' Glasgow and its Environs*, 1891

BLACKLOCK & MACARTHUR'S
Well-known 'STAG' BRAND

WHITE LEAD, WHITE ZINC, RED LEAD, PAINTS IN PASTE AND LIQUID STATE.

All kinds of Dry Colours, Varnishes, Etc., suitable for Railway Companies, Shipbuilders, Coachbuilders, Painters, and Decorators' Uses.

Paint, Burning and Lubricating Oils, Turpentine, Greases, Tallow, Chemicals, Liquid Sheep-marking Paint, Wool-Wash Powder, Packed suitably for Home or Export.

CONTRACTORS TO HOME AND FOREIGN GOVERNMENTS.

Address—171 to 173 WEST STREET, TRADESTON, GLASGOW.

425-3 *Telephone No. 541   Telegrams 'BLACARTH,' Glasgow.   Exhibit No. 804, Class XII.*

The Mitchell Library

Blacklock & MacArthur of Tradeston, advertising in 1888

Much of the highly decorative building of the Clydesdale Paint, Oil and Colour Works still exists, complete with its sculpted stag's head trademark.

The following extract, from a novel by A J Cronin, is used here for its description of domestic circumstances in the industrial streets, although it appears to belong on the other side of the river. Cronin, although he depicted Glasgow in several novels, often re-invented both the names and the geography. Thus 'Winton' is undoubtedly Glasgow, but 'Gorbielaw' could be one of any number of districts.

The habitat of my Uncle Leo was a four-storey warehouse somewhat peculiarly named Templar's Hall and was situated in that unsalubrious district of Winton known as Gorbielaw. The building, which occupied one quarter of two mean, narrow cobbled streets, was old and in poor repair with the side windows plastered over and painted a dingy black, but as it stood in the centre of the city, adjacent to Argyle Street and convenient for the docks, it presumably had for my uncle advantages of a commercial nature.

As a residence it had less to offer. The top floor, consisting of a long dark passage with a great many rooms opening off on either side, served as the living quarters. However, as I had arrived late the night before I had as yet no idea of the nature of these rooms, only that my own, furnished with an iron bed, a washstand and a burst cane chair, was at the far end of the corridor, and the kitchen, where a sort of general servant to my uncle, Annie Tobin, had given me bread and cheese for my supper, at the other.

from *A Song of Sixpence*, A J Cronin, 1964

For: Citizens Theatre; Sheriff Court; College of Nautical Studies; Central Mosque

BRIDGE STREET station, actually situated at No 57 Eglinton Street, lies on the edge of what was quintessential Gorbals, a few hundred yards south of the Clyde.

Bridge Street had been the location of Glasgow's first real mainline railway terminus in 1840, before Glasgow Central Station on the north bank of the Clyde was sufficiently extended in 1906.

The station facade was an architectural masterpiece, and the travelling public had to wait over thirty years to see anything which could rival it. Bridge Street was a romantic product of the railway optimism of the early 1840s. Just getting to Bridge Street had involved an engineering feat well described in *The Railway Times* for 4 July 1840:

'The railway is carried over four streets by centre arches of 46ft span [14m.], with side passages. Over King Street by a bridge of stone, and over Nelson Street, Wallace Street and Cook Street by bridges of iron. In addition to these, it is carried over 49 arches of brick [over 5 million bricks were used] of about 26ft [7.8m.] span; all of these in a distance of about 550 yards [504m.]. Had the terminus been at Cook Street, the saving in property and building would have been great. The expense however will be in some degree compensated by the cellarage which so many arches afford.'

from *Glasgow Stations*, Colin Johnston and John R Hume, 1979

45

Train journeys from Bridge Street, and from Glasgow Central through Bridge Street, are well-described in a number of novels:

It was raining more heavily as he hurried along Argyle Street. The muddy street was shining in the lights. Several times the wheels of the passing buses splashed him, for in his hurry he tried to keep to the less-crowded side of the pavement. Filthy urchins were calling an evening paper. Hucksters of various kinds were calling their wares. Fresh herrings. Mussels. Caller oysters. Here and there at the turn of a side-street, a barrow of vegetables. John Anderson's Royal Polytechnic was a blaze of light.

Now down Jamaica Street and across the Glasgow Bridge. It was raining heavily. He bent his head as the rain struck against his face. A steamer boomed in the darkness. Above the sound of the traffic he could hear the beat of paddles as another steamer pounded itself against the force of the black, muddy river into position along the quayside of the Broomielaw. Its bow was almost under the bridge.

But here was Clyde Place and the Bridge Street Station steps. In a moment more he was under shelter.

In a few minutes he would be out of it all. And a good thing. For he was a countryman, and he was going back to the country.

The rain lashed in bitter bursts against the windows of his carriage whenever the train was free from the covering protection of the station. The raindrops glistened and sparkled on the panes as the train, working its way outwards across the points, moved past street lamps and lighted shops and houses.

from *Wax Fruit*, Guy McCrone, 1947

T & R Annan & Sons

The tracks and platforms of Bridge Street Station, c.1870

He found a corner seat in a carriage; and, as the train went out, joggling at first over crossing lines, he wanted to dance to that dancing sound. The train rumbled across the bridge; and it was, tonight, a rumble like the roll of kettle-drums. Far below was the river, the deep-dyed fuliginous river, showing dropped gold from masthead lights in the midst of its mugginess, showing swirling streaks, oily, rouge-like – slimy purples, shuddery deep, blacky greens. A light slid under the bridge. Wharf lights suddenly, if dimly, showed that it was a light on a launch that, as it sped along, disturbed the stream into a multitude of broken ripples.

Then the river was left behind. 'Bridge Street! Bridge Street!' – and they paused a moment, and were off again. As the train rattled up to the high-level platform at Eglinton Street, a white-painted train screamed parallel with them, and rushed on upon the low-level, emitting sparks, showing its streak of white with a blaze of lit windows, each going out suddenly, like the closing of a telescope, as it tore into the tunnel there, leaving only coils of grey smoke and steam in the empty station.

from *Justice of the Peace*, Frederick Niven, 1914

IRATE PASSENGER.—" Hoo lang am I tae staun here ? "
CIVIL PORTER.—" Just as lang's you like."
I. P.—" But, when are we to start ? "
C. P.—" After the engine gets a wet."
I. P.—" Lucky dog ; I wish I could get the same."

The Mitchell Library

Dry railway humour: a cartoon from 'Quiz' of June 1898

The 'coils of grey smoke and steam' evoke the smells of steam coal and hot oil which were the – not always unpleasant – fundamentals of confinement in a low-level station. Less pleasant however than the glass-house grandeur of a larger station:

A porter had seized her black box and was marching down with the main stream to the entrance. Phoebe looked up at the flares of gas burning in the station, although the daylight was not altogether gone. Suddenly she realised that she was walking under great roofs of glass! She could count three of them! She was walking in a great glass-house! They were through the barrier. What a wide stair leading down into the street! Arthur said it was Clyde Place. And there was the Clyde! He called her attention to two great steamers, their paddle-boxes gleaming with golden paint, lying against the other bank. That was the Broomielaw, where the steamers were. One of them, he said, went all the way to Ireland.

A boy no bigger than herself but much older-looking came forward and tugged at the glossy skip of his dirty cap. He pointed to a little flat hand-cart. 'Tak' yer trunk, sir?'

from *Wax Fruit*, Guy McCrone, 1947

As other passengers entered he glanced at each, wondering if he or she might be a neighbour. When the train started he looked out of the window, as interested as a boy in the moving panorama. A pleasure steamer had just moved out from the Broomielaw to the middle of the stream. The Irish boat lay beyond, and a host of ships of all nations further below.

The train slid past the backs of old tenements, where sometimes, when passing on the track near them, one had an intimate view of poverty-stricken domesticity, and then it began to race the red trams in Eglinton Street. Not very interesting. John picked up *The Glasgow Herald*, which he had neatly folded. Every morning, like other prosperous Glasgow men, he cast his first glance at the newspaper down the column headed, 'Deaths', as if there might be an appetising delight, a zest to attack the day's work, in seeing how many of his friends and acquaintances had died.

from *Mungo* George Woden, 1932

A more compassionate traveller, and one who ventured into the unfamiliar threat of Eglinton Street on foot, nevertheless imagined the tramcar as escape vehicle. . .

One evening Mansie decided to walk home instead of taking the tramcar as usual. He had been in the office all day giving an account of his last quarter's work and going over the possibilities of opening up new custom during the coming weeks; the manager had been very pleased with his report, but Mansie felt cramped and a little stifled after sitting all day in the poky office – the manager had actually insisted on sending out for dinner – and now he wanted to stretch his legs. And besides he was curious to find out how Eglinton Street would strike him now after such a long time, for passing through it in the tramcar every evening was quite a different thing from walking from end to end of it on foot. Months and months it must have been since he had done that; not more than once or twice since he had been taken from the office and put on the road.

He crossed the Jamaica Bridge. Dusk was falling and the lamps were being lit; they ran in two straight rows up the slightly rising street, and those

The Mitchell Library

A fine Annan photograph from about 1870 shows an almost empty Bridge Street, with a horse-cab approaching the superb, pedimented Doric columns of the early Bridge Street Station

in the distance hung in a soft moony haze that was almost fairy-like. The pavement was damp and sticky, though there had been no rain, and now it seemed to him that it had always been like that. After passing through on the tramcar, too, one felt uncomfortably near the ground down here, as though walking along the bottom of a gully which was always slightly damp, while a little above the level of one's head ran a smooth and clean high road. When a tramcar sailed by with all its lights on he felt tempted to run after it.

Astonishing the number of dirty squalling children that were down here, down here the whole time by all appearances, for you never saw them anywhere else, perhaps they never got up at all, poor little beggars. And the way they yelled and screamed was enough to scare you; wasn't like a human sound at all. Yet you never heard them when you were passing on the tramcar.

from *Poor Tom*, Edwin Muir, 1932

The next extract is a few streets transposed from its own setting, but is a sympathetic depiction of life in the 'solid cliffs of masonry'.

The close known as 150 South Wellington Street was like thousands of other Glasgow slum closes, a short, narrow walled-in passage leading up to three landings and through to a grassless earthen or broken-bricked back-court, with its small, mean communal wash-house and open, insanitary midden. In such back-courts the women of the tenements, after taking their weekly turn in the wash-house, hang out the family washing and take it in dried with sunshine or strong seawind and half-dirtied with industrial smoke and grime. They are the only playground of many thousands of the city's children, where the youngsters play football and children's games, climb on the midden and wash-house roofs and escape death or injury from the perilous traffic of the streets.

They look like tunnels cut through solid cliffs of masonry, these closes, and in the slums are decorated in the crudest style. Halfway up their walls are painted a stone or chocolate colour which is separated from whitewash by a stencilled border of another shade. There are often great holes in the walls of these closes, left unplastered or, if filled in, left unpainted and presenting unsightly daubs of crudely plastered cement. As the walls are for long periods unrefreshed with new paint, the old paint cracks and peels and the dingy whitewash flakes and falls before factors will spend money on property renovation. Many tenement dwellers live indifferent to all this ugliness and those with some spirit, who are angered by it all, lose heart in their long, unequal struggle against the tight-fistedness of factors, and live on and die in homes too narrow for fuller life, from which it seems there is no escape. These closes, badly lit, with their dangerous broken-stepped stairs, often filthy and malodorous, smelling of catspiss and drunkards' spew, have been

The City Archives

Cumberland Street, Hutchesontown c.1955, when it was still safe to stroll in the middle of the road

for generations of Glaswegians the favourite, and for thousands, the only, courting-place, and many hurried, unhappy marriages have originated there. 'Stonnin' at the close' or 'closemooth' is a social habit of tenement dwellers and at all hours lone individuals lounge, staring vacantly.

from *Dance of the Apprentices*, Edward Gaitens 1948

One of the best-known novels which is set in and around the old Gorbals is not by any means the best or most truly evocative:

On that particular Thursday evening of 1924 Johnnie had left the open-air gymnasium in Glasgow Green and was on his way home when he met Lizzie Ramsay outside the 'Coffin Building.' Frazer's Hair Factory, which stands opposite St Luke's School and Chapel in Govan Street, Gorbals, is a brick building of three storeys with a coffin-like bulge at the end nearest Commercial Road. Govan Street itself narrows into a bottle-neck to accommodate the bulge of the factory. Johnnie, walking along the street a few minutes after five o' clock, noticed that the red brick of the Coffin Building had warmed to a coppery glow in the sunset and the curved tramlines stretched ahead of him like streaks of gold. The rush of the tenement-dwellers was over at that hour and, rounding the bulge, he over-took Lizzie Ramsay on her way home from work in a West End bakery.

from *No Mean City*, Alexander McArthur and H Kingsley Long, 1935

The People's Palace

The long-lamented Gorbals Cross, c.1900

The Herald

One of the last photographs of a Gorbals street-scene, in the early 1960s: a good stand-in for Jeff Torrington's Scobie Street

A much more poignant, memorable, witty (and prize-winning) novel is set in the Gorbals at that period in the 1960s when the area was being systematically bulldozed (in preparation for a redevelopment which was as infamously ill-designed and badly constructed as the original 'solid cliffs of masonry' had been neglected):

> Fires fuelled by wooden beams burned in cleared sites. Rubble was being trucked from busted gable ends and demolishers worked in a fume of dust and smoke. You would've thought that the Ruskies had finally lobbed over one of their big megaton jobs: streets wiped out, landscapes pulverised. On a gutted site near a fire that drizzled sparks on him, a greybeard sat in a lopsided armchair, placidly smoking his pipe. I nudged Eddie and pointed to the old guy. He spared the greybeard a cold glance then returned his attention to the windscreen through which could be seen advancing streets shorn of their pavements by the snow, and of their buildings by the Hammer. It was inaccurate to call them 'streets' anymore for they looked like a series of bleak airstrips.
>
> Most of the old Gorbals had been levelled by now. Housing Planners had taken up their slum-erasers and rubbed out the people who'd lived there. Some original specks still clung to the Redevelopment blueprints but these would be blown away shortly. In Scobie Street, for instance, a few commercial concerns continued to function: there was Nelly Kemp's fag'n paper shop; Joe Fiducci's barbering joint; The Salty Dog Saloon (my local watering hole);

and Shug Wylie's public lavatory (Men Only) which stood out in the middle of the street almost directly opposite the Planet Cinema. The movie house was bracketed by the defunct O'Leary's betting shop and the derelict Blue Pacific Cafe, mention of which is made in local bard John Scobie's 'Ode to a Flea Ranch', where he described the kinema as being 'A crackit planet betwixt the deil and the deep blue sea. . .'

from *Swing Hammer Swing!* Jeff Torrington, 1992

The City Improvement Trust had swept away much of the worst domestic property between 1871 and 1891, but the Comprehensive Development Area demolitions of the 1960s were badly thought out and the ill-designed concrete slabs, which were dumped in windswept desolation, only denied the possibility of sensitive rehabilitation.

The final scenes which relate to the Bridge Street vicinity come from that well-loved Ealing Studios production, *The Maggie* and involve the unlikely collision of Captain MacTaggart's disreputable puffer with the tunnel of the Glasgow District Subway!

> MLS SHOOTING DOWN ON *MAGGIE* CHUGGING OUT INTO CLYDE, NIGHT.
> MS WEE BOY LOOKING WORRIED.
> MS CAPTAIN IN WHEELHOUSE, WITH MATE DOWN BELOW ON DECK. ALSO ENGINEMAN. WEE BOY COMES INTO SHOT.

> WEE BOY (*coming into shot, to SKIPPER*): Captain, sir?
> SKIPPER (*to WEE BOY*): Aye?
> WEE BOY (*timidly, to SKIPPER*):Is it no' about low tide?
> SKIPPER (*to WEE BOY*): Aye.
> WEE BOY (*to SKIPPER, off*): With all this cargo on board are we no runnin' a bit low in the water?
> SKIPPER (*off, to WEE BOY*): Aye, but . . .
> WEE BOY (*to SKIPPER, off*): Well, I mean, sir, is it no a bit . . . dangerous going down this part of the river where there's . . .
> ENGINEMAN (*to WEE BOY*): Haud your whist! Whit dae you know aboot it . . .
> SKIPPER (*to WEE BOY*): Ye're no the captain yet, laddie.
> WEE BOY (*protesting*): I didna . . .   I was just . . .
> MATE (*to WEE BOY*): You're gettin' far too cheeky. Now away forward an' make us some tea.
> MS WEE BOY TURNING ROUND TO GLANCE AT REST OF CREW.
> LS *MAGGIE* GOING DOWN CLYDE TOWARDS BRIDGE. THERE IS A CRASH.
> MS WEE BOY DUCKING.
> MS ENGINEMAN AND MATE TUMBLING OVER.
> MCS SKIPPER HOLDING ON TO WHEEL TO PULL HIMSELF UP.

HE LOOKS OUT AND TURNS ROUND TO CAMERA, REACTING.
DISSOLVE TO
MLS EXTERIOR, WORLD AIRWAYS BUILDING.
DISSOLVE TO
MS INTERIOR OF MARSHALL'S VERY BUSY OFFICE. MISS PETERS IS
    ON PHONE F/G. MARSHALL'S OWN OFFICE TO RIGHT. DOOR
    PARTLY OPEN WITH PUSEY JUST INSIDE.
MISS PETERS (answering telephone): Hullo.
MARSHALL'S VOICE (off): And you know it very well.
(Marshall's voice continues b/g but is inaudible).
MISS PETERS (into telephone): Just a moment. (TO PUSEY) Mr Campbell
    on the line, Mr Pusey.
PUSEY (taking phone, to MISS PETERS): Thank you.
(Into telephone) Hallo, Mr Campbell. I was rather anxious so I thought
    I'd phone you. I trust the cargo got away all right?
Pardon? Why, the cargo on the boat of course.
What boat?
Why, the boat I chartered yesterday.
MS INTERIOR OF CAMPBELL'S OFFICE. HE IS ON PHONE, HIS
    SECRETARY JUST BEHIND, CSS OFFICER IN LITTLE OFFICE B/G,
    ALL LOOKING VERY AMUSED.
CAMPBELL (into telephone): You found a boat then?
PUSEY'S VOICE (over telephone): Why . . .
CAMPBELL (into telephone): Well done.
MS PUSEY ON PHONE. MISS PETERS REACTS TO HIS TONE.
    BUSY SCENE.
PUSEY (into telephone): Found a boat? (to MISS PETERS) This man's
    quite impossible.
MS CAMPBELL ON PHONE. HIS SECRETARY AND OTHER
    OFFICERS B/G.
CAMPBELL (to his SECRETARY): This lad is off his head. (to PUSEY)
    Aye. You made arrangements with whom? MacTaggart!
JAMIESON (to CAMPBELL): MacTaggart? But – it's him there's been all
    the fuss about down at the Broomielaw!
CAMPBELL (swivelling round in his chair,as his SECRETARY starts
    laughing): But . . .
MS PUSEY ON PHONE. MISS PETERS, ETC.
PUSEY (peevishly, into telephone): Mr Campbell, in all my experience I . . .
MS CAMPBELL, JAMIESON, AND SECRETARY, ALL LAUGHING
    OVER NEWSPAPER.
CAMPBELL (breaking into roars of laughter, into telephone): And it's still
    there?!
Oh, Mr Pusey, MacTaggart has nothing to do with our organisation.
He's master of an old puffer.

The puffer *Maggie.*

CS PUSEY ON PHONE. MISS PETERS BEHIND. BUSY SCENE.

PUSEY (into telephone): No.

Oh, no.

CAMPBELL, ETC. AS BEFORE.

CAMPBELL (into telephone): And you mean to say you put your cargo on his boat? *(Laughter)* Well, the chances are you've seen the last of it.

CS PUSEY, AS BEFORE.

PUSEY (into telephone): That isn't possible.

LOUD LAUGHTER ON PHONE

MARSHALL's VOICE (on intercom): Send Pusey in.

MISS PETERS (taking telephone, as laughter continues to come through): Hullo. Hullo.

MLS SHOOTING ACROSS MARSHALL'S OFFICE AT PUSEY, VERY NERVOUS.

PUSEY (very nervously, to MARSHALL, off): And he – gave me his signature.

MARSHALL (off, to PUSEY): Well?

PUSEY (to MARSHALL, off): He signed the inventory.

MARSHALL (off, to PUSEY): So?

PUSEY (to MARSHALL, off): So naturally, I – chartered the boat.

MARSHALL (off, to PUSEY): And?

PUSEY (to MARSHALL, off): They weren't who they said they were.

And Campbell says the cargo isn't on the boat – it's in Glasgow.

And the man you spoke to – he hasn't a boat at all but something called a puffer.

MARSHALL DISCLOSED.

PUSEY (contd. to MARSHALL, disclosed): And instead of being well on its way to Kiltarra it's stuck on the Subway and not even the right boat.

MCS MARSHALL. HE TAKES OFF SPECTACLES.

MARSHALL (to PUSEY, off): Just let me get one thing straight. You say a boat is stuck on a subway?

SHOUTING AND HUBBUB.

MLS SHOOTING DOWN ON *MAGGIE* STUCK IN MIDDLE OF CLYDE. CROWDS ON BANKS CHEER AND LAUGH.

SKIPPER (to RIVER POLICEMAN): I was sailing this river while you were eating saps.

POLICEMAN (to SKIPPER): The Subway lies under the river at this point.

SKIPPER (to POLICEMAN): The Subway is a menace to navigation!

MS *MAGGIE* STUCK.

POLICEMAN (to SKIPPER): . . . and all ships are . . .

You had no right to put out at that state of the tide. You may have damaged the Sub . . .

SKIPPER (to POLICEMAN): What about the damage to my ship?!

55

MS SHOOTING DOWN ON PRESS BOAT. FRAZER STANDS.

FRAZER (*to MACTAGGART, off*): Captain MacTaggart?

MLS SHOOTING OVER PRESS BOAT AT MACTAGGART ON *MAGGIE*.
POLICE BOAT B/G/

SKIPPER (*to FRAZER*): Aye.

FRAZER (*to SKIPPER*): I'm from the *Evening News*. Would you care to
make a statement?

SKIPPER (*to FRAZER*): You can say that I'm considering bringing an
action!

from the post production script of *The Maggie*, Ealing Films/UGC (UK):
screenplay by William Rose, 1954

The Herald

'You say a boat is stuck on a Subway?' The film-makers' stranded Maggie
had to be a mock-up to appease the authorities

GOVAN CROSS
IBROX
CESSNOCK
KINNING PARK
SHIELDS ROAD
WEST STREET
BRIDGE STREET

ST ENOCH

BUCHANAN STREET
COWCADDENS
ST GEORGE'S CROSS
KELVINBRIDGE
HILLHEAD
KELVIN HALL
PARTICK

For: Travel Centre; Bus Interchange; Central Station; Princes Square; St Enoch Shopping Centre; Tron Theatre; Clyde Walkway; Suspension Bridge; St Andrew's R.C. Cathedral

BEFORE THERE was a St Enoch Station, or even a St Enoch Square, the early city of Glasgow was greatly admired by its visitors:

Now, let us descend to describe the splendour and gaity of this city of Glasgow, which surpasseth most, if not all the corporations in Scotland. Here it is you may observe four large fair streets, modell'd, as it were, into a spacious quadrant; in the centre whereof their market-place is fix'd; near unto which stands a stately tolbooth, a very sumptuous, regulated, uniform fabrick, large and lofty, most industriously and artificially carved from the very foundation to the superstructure, to the great admiration of strangers and travellers. But this state-house, or tolbooth, is their western prodigy, infinitely excelling the model and usual built of town-halls; and is, without exception, the paragon of beauty in the west; whose compeer is no where to be found in the north, should you rally the rarities of all the corporations in Scotland.

In the next place, we are to consider the merchants and traders in this eminent Glasgow, whose store-houses and ware-houses are stuft with merchandize, as their shops swell big with foreign commodities, and returns from France, and other remote parts, where they have agents and factors to correspond, and inrich their maritime ports, whose charter exceeds all the charters in Scotland; which is a considerable advantage to the city-inhabitants, because blest with privileges as large, nay, larger than any other

57

corporation. Moreover, they dwell in the face of France, and a free trade, as I formerly told you. Nor is this all, for the staple of their country consists of linens, friezes, furs, tartans, pelts, hides, tallow, skins, and various other small manufactures and commodities, not comprehended in this breviat. Besides, I should remind you, that they generally exceed in good French wines, as they naturally superabound with fish and fowl; some meat does well with their drink.

from an account by Richard Franck in 1656

The streets of Glasgo are large and handsome, as if belonging to a new town; but the houses are only of wood, ornamented with carving. Here live several rich shopkeepers. As soon as I had passed the bridge, I came to the entry of two broad streets. In the first is a large building, being the hospital of the merchants[1], and farther on the market-place, and town-hall[2], built with large stones, with a square tower being the town clock-house; under which is the guard-house, as in all the towns of consequence in England. Although Glasgo has no other fortification, that does not prevent it from being very strong, for towards the east side it is elevated upon a scarped rock, the foot whereof is washed by a little river[3], very convenient to that part of the town through which it passes. I lodged in this fine large street. The son of the owner of the house, being then studying philosophy at the university, conducted me everywhere, in order to point out to me what was most remarkable in the town.

from an account by Jorevin de Rocheford in 1661

Tobias Smollett is regarded as one of the founders of the English Novel. Born in the Vale of Leven, Smollett was also a surgeon, journalist, pamphleteer and travel-writer. One of his two greatest novels takes the form of a series of wonderfully descriptive letters written by a party of friends on a rambling tour of Britain in 1771. Glasgow was one of the highlights.

I am so far happy as to have seen Glasgow, which, to the best of my re-collection and judgement, is one of the prettiest towns in Europe; and, without all doubt, is one of the most flourishing in Great Britain. In short, it is a perfect bee-hive in point of industry. It stands partly on a partial declivity; but the greatest part of it is in a plain, watered by the river Clyde. The streets are straight, open, airy, and well paved; and the houses lofty and well built of hewn stone. At the upper end of the town, there is a venerable cathedral, that may be compared with York-minster or West-minster; and, about the middle of the descent from this to the Cross, is the college, a respectable pile of a building, with all manner of accommodation for the professors and students,

[1] Hutcheson's Hospital [2] The Tolbooth [3] The Molendinar Burn

including an elegant library, and a[n] observatory well provided with astronomical instruments. The number of inhabitants is said to amount to thirty thousand; and marks of opulence and independency appear in every quarter of this commercial city, which, however, is not without its inconveniences and defects. The water of their public pumps is generally hard and brackish, an imperfection the less excusable, as the river Clyde runs by their doors, in the lower part of the town; and there are rivulets and springs above the cathedral sufficient to fill a large reservoir with excellent water, which might thence be distributed to all the different parts of the city.

It is of more consequence to consult the health of the inhabitants in this article, than to employ so much attention in beautifying their town with new streets, squares, and churches. Another defect, not so easily remedied, is the shallowness of the river, which will not float vessels of any burthen within ten or twelve miles of the city; so that the merchants are obliged to load and unload their ships at Greenock or Port-Glasgow, situated about fourteen miles nearer the mouth of the Frith, where it is about two miles broad.

letter from Matt Bramble in *Humphrey Clinker,* Tobias Smollett, 1771

An undoubtedly real visitor was the reactionary Dr Samuel Johnson, who made an extended visit to Scotland in 1773 with his friend and biographer James Boswell. Even the cantankerous Johnson was pleased with his visit to Glasgow, where they stayed 'in high glee' at the Saracen's Head:

To describe a city so much frequented as Glasgow, is unnecessary. The prosperity of its commerce appears by the greatness of many private houses, and a general appearance of wealth.

from *A Journey to the Western Islands of Scotland,* Samuel Johnson,1774

It has to be pointed out that the 18th century Saracen's Head was a fairly grand place, as an advertisement at the time of its opening made clear:

Robert Tennant, who formerly kept the White Hart Inn, without the Gallowgate Port, is removed to the Saracen's Head, where the port formerly stood.

He takes this opportunity to acquaint all ladies and gentlemen, that at the desire of the magistrates of Glasgow, he has built a convenient and handsome new inn, agreeable to a plan given him, containing 36 fine rooms, now fit to receive lodgers. The bed-chambers are all separate, none of them entering through another, and so contrived that there is no need of going out of doors to get to them. The beds are all very good, clean, and free from bugs. There are very good stables for horses, and a pump well in the yard for watering them, with a shade within the said yard for coaches, chaises, or other wheel carriages.

The Glasgow Journal, October 1755

The Saracen's Head Inn drawn as it appeared in 1885, possibly still free from bugs!

James Boswell, in his own account of the Glasgow visit, ticked Johnson off for an earlier flippant remark about the city:

> The professors of the university being informed of our arrival, Dr Stevenson, Dr Reid, and Mr Anderson, breakfasted with us. Mr Anderson accompanied us while Dr Johnson viewed this beautiful city. He had told me, that one day in London, when Dr Adam Smith was boasting of it, he turned to him and said, 'Pray, sir, have you ever seen Brentford?' – This was surely a strong instance of his impatience, and spirit of contradiction. I put him in mind of it today, while he expressed his admiration of the elegant buildings, and whispered him, 'Don't you feel some remorse?'
>
> from *Journal of a Tour to The Hebrides with Samuel Johnson LLD*, James Boswell,1785

Another entirely real visitor, who kept a detailed diary of a similar tour of Britain, was Dorothy Wordsworth, who accompanied her brother William and his fellow poet Coleridge. While they were ecstatic at the sight of Loch Lomond, their visit to Glasgow occurred on a dreich day:

> *Tuesday, August 23rd 1803* – A cold morning. Walked to the bleaching-ground [Glasgow Green], a large field bordering on the Clyde, the banks of which are perfectly flat, and the general face of the country is nearly so in the neighbourhood of Glasgow. This field, the whole summer through, is covered with women of all ages, children, and young girls spreading out their linen, and watching it while it bleaches. The scene must be very cheerful on a fine day, but it rained when we were there, and though there was linen spread out

in all parts, and great numbers of women and girls were at work, yet there would have been many more on a fine day, and they would have appeared happy, instead of stupid and cheerless. In the middle of the field is a wash-house, wither the inhabitants of this large town, rich and poor, send or carry their linen to be washed. There are two very large rooms, with each a cistern in the middle for hot water; and all round the rooms are benches for the women to set their tubs upon. Both the rooms were crowded with washers; there might be a hundred, or two, or even three; for it is not easy to form an accurate notion of so great a number; however, the rooms were large, and they were both full. It was amusing to see so many women, arms, head and face all in motion, all busy in an ordinary household employment, in which we are accustomed to see, at the most, only three or four women employed in one place. The women were very civil. I learnt from them the regulations of the house; but I have forgotten the particulars. The substance of them is, that 'so much' is to be paid for each tub of water, 'so much' for a tub, and the privilege of washing for a day, and, 'so much' to the general overlookers of the linen, when it is left to be bleached. An old man and woman have this office, who were walking about, two melancholy figures.

The shops at Glasgow are large, and like London shops, and we passed by the largest coffee-room I ever saw. You look across the piazza of the Exchange, and see to the end of the coffee-room, where there is a circular window, the width of the room. Perhaps there might be thirty gentlemen sitting on the circular bench of the window, each reading a newspaper. They had the appearance of figures in a fantoccine, or men seen at the extremity of the opera-house, diminished into puppets.

from *Recollections of a Tour made in Scotland, AD 1803*, Dorothy Wordsworth

The mediaeval city centre eventually spread, initially along Argyle Street, to encompass what was to become St Enoch Square.

Argyle Street in 1124 was the road to Dumbarton Castle. On 27 July 1783, R Browne, perfumer, Argyle Street, advertises that he supplies 'genuine violet powder for the hair, of a neat, elegant and cheerful kind': said to be the first mention of Argyle Street.

Robert Carrick, of the Ship Bank, lived in the second flat above the bank offices, in a house on the north side down to 1821.

Lord Provost Patrick Colquhoun (of the Luss family) had a house in Argyle Street before he removed to London.

About 1828 George Douglass, plumber, Virginia Street, 'was the first who put plate glass into windows in his property in Argyle Street, near Buchanan Street. It was considered generally a great risk and monstrous extravagance.'

from *Glasgow Streets and Places*, James Muir, CA, 1899

Argyle Street, which till 1777 was known as West Street, has been of late almost entirely rebuilt in varied, but generally pleasing and dignified, style. This street, which is very long, and continued under different names right through the city from east to west, a distance of fully four miles, is very crowded at all times, and reminds one of central parts of London for bustle and activity, although private carriages are not so numerous. A branch from the Caledonian Railway is about to be carried out, burrowing underneath Argyle Street and Trongate, so connecting the extreme eastern and western parts of Glasgow, namely Dalmarnock and Maryhill.

from *Strattens' Glasgow and its Environs*, 1891

St Enoch Square is reached by crossing Argyle Street, and is well-known to Londoners as the terminus of the Midland Railway (really Glasgow and South Western, from Carlisle). Not long ago, with its quiet parish Church, which still remains, a few trees and shrubs in the central Square growing over a very ancient burying-place, and with its circle of sedate villas, it seemed a solemn, dreamy place, fit to commemorate the virtues of good St Taneu, who, as we have seen, was the mother of the holy St Mungo.

from *Strattens' Glasgow and its Environs*, 1891

The old Square, which had been opened in 1782, was soon to be disturbed, but its tranquillity also survives in fiction:

The Sanderson Institute stood on the far side of the river, in an almost forgotten part of the city, between the Pensioners' Hospice and the ancient St Enoch's Church. It was a quiet district, and the gardens in St Enoch's Square gave to it a country look. Rain had fallen the night before, a soft spring rain, and as I made my way along the flagged pavement of Old George Street there was a smell of sap and young grass in the air.

A warm breeze came from the river and swung the buds of the tall elm trees where the sparrows were chirping. All at once the cold grip of winter seemed to have relaxed and the moist earth, opening to the sunshine, gave forth a heady sweetness that filled me with longing, with an ineffable yearning, that was like a pain.

from *Shannon's Way*, A J Cronin, 1948

But the railways were coming, and the 'country look' was on the way out. However, the great railway terminus that was to come to St Enoch Square was, of its kind, superb.

In the city centre there was endless difficulty over the acquisition of land. The City of Glasgow Union Railway's fine plans for an elaborate station in St Enoch Square were delayed by resident tenants who refused to vacate their properties. The company stopped the branch short at Dunlop Street where a temporary four-platform station was established, while the fight for ground continued. It was to be six years before St Enoch came into use. It was all that the CGU had promised. With its hotel (the largest in Scotland) it was a great gothic castle of a place. Passengers who alighted there on 1 May 1876 after having travelled from St Pancras by the first train over the Settle and Carlisle route must have seen something of Midland splendour in St Enoch's glazed arch, 504 ft long, 80 ft high and with a clear span of 198 ft.

Glasgow's first really great terminal station received the royal accolade, and a ceremonial opening, on 17 October 1876 when the Prince and Princess of Wales arrived in the royal train. In 1883 the station and its approach lines were taken over by the Glasgow and South Western Railway and St Enoch became the headquarters of that railway.

from A Regional History of the Railways of Great Britain, Vol. 6, Scotland, The Lowlands and The Borders,
John Thomas, 1971

St Enoch Hotel is not only the largest in Scotland, but ranks third in point of dimensions of those in the United Kingdom. It is surpassed only by the Langham Hotel and Midland Hotel, London. Externally its appearance is very attractive: internally it has been carefully planned and furnished to promote the complete comfort of the occupants. It is six storeys high. In the basement floor, below the level of St Enoch Square, is the kitchen, 85ft long by 32 ft wide, with ceilings 20ft high. In close proximity to the kitchen are ranges of larders and pantries, ice presses, meat safes, etc. A lift furnishes the means of communication between the basement floor and those above it.

Speaking tubes and electric bells are extended into the kitchen. On the

Aberdeen University

St Enoch Station and Hotel, photographed before the arrival of
The Subway

floor above are the servants' apartments, laundry, etc. They are accessible by entrances from Howard Street and St Enoch Square. On the ground floor, the visitor, entering by a neat pillared Gothic porch, finds a spacious hall, high-roofed, finely lighted, and beautifully furnished. Broad easy flights of stairs and passages lead to other parts of the building. By the principal staircase, which has been formed of stone and iron, treated in ornamental style, passage is obtained to the first floor.

The largest apartment is the coffee-room. Adjoining it are the drawing-room and music-room. On the same floor are the billiard-room, general sitting-room, private dining-room, and several suites of apartments, comprising several bedrooms, bath-rooms, etc. On the upper storeys are apartments and bedrooms for visitors. In the attics are airy comfortable servants' apartments.

from History of the Glasgow & South Western Railway, 1880

St Enoch Station was the first building in Glasgow (just ahead of the main Post Office) to be lit by electricity. The opulence which the station and hotel offered became famous, and facilities equalled the best available internationally.

Another [distinction] can be drawn between those [facilities] provided for the ordinary passengers and those for the extraordinary. Many stations had unusual offices. Windsor had a special waiting-room for Queen Victoria, New Delhi one for the Viceroy – occupied for several years more recently by a slighted Indian aristocratic lady. At Ottawa there were special rooms laid aside for government officials and politicians. Washington Union had a special retiring-room and reception-room for the President. There were also mortuary chambers, perhaps anticipating assassinations – remembering the fate of President Garfield at an earlier Washington station. A few had special rooms for funeral parties. At Glasgow St. Enoch there was a room in which commercial travellers could show off their sample cases in comfort and privacy.

Washing, shaving, and hairdressing facilities were often installed to accompany new conveniences and they frequently earned praise, as for instance those at Glasgow St Enoch's:

'A special word of praise is due to the toilet rooms adjoining the lavatories on No 1 platform. These are "run" by Mr Taynton, and the accommodation comprises two handsomely fitted-up rooms, in which palms and ferns make a very attractive show against the white-glazed tiles.

In these two rooms no less than 11 unshorn and unkempt passengers can be operated on at once, there being a staff of thirteen in all. The dozen or so circular brushes which go to make this department complete are revolved by an electric motor.' [The Railway Magazine, 1904].

from The Railway Station, a Social History, J Richards and J MacKenzie, 1986

Not much hope for a latter-day Mr Taynton in railway stations these days. Although, it might be depressingly possible to imagine an over-priced 'Mister Beardie' chain of day-glo franchises operated by under-paid youths working oppressive split shifts. Let's hope just for a few trains. . .

As she came through from the booking-hall she found herself under the gigantic glass arch of the new railway station of St Enoch's. For a moment she looked about her with curiosity. It was one of the sights of Glasgow, this great station which was barely yet completed, and its novelty caught her interest.

Her train was waiting. Lucy found an empty first-class carriage, wrapped her travelling-rug about her and sat down. There was a Friday-night anima-tion about other travellers. Week-ending was coming much into vogue. Business men who could afford to live in the mansion houses that heretofore had been occupied by the gentry, were beginning more and more to gather their friends about them from Friday night to Monday morning, to forget for two days of the week at least that they were men of business, and to ape the ways of the people whose houses they were increasingly coming to occupy.

Presently the train moved off, slowly puffing its way out of the great new station into the evening, rounding the old steeple of the Merchants' House, crossing a wind-swept, leaden Clyde, passing the growing suburbs on the south side of the river, and speeding out into the open country.

from *Wax Fruit*, Guy McCrone, 1947

Kelvingrove Art Gallery

Third Class, *a fine ink drawing by A S Boyd captures some choice travelling companions*

65

It has to be said that, in common with most of the country's railway stations, the wonderful St Enoch became a neglected jewel. Even the latter-day squalor has been brilliantly recorded:

St Enoch was Glasgow's answer to London's St Pancras. The accent was on gothic functionalism, and although there was little stained glass on show, steam and smoke were quickly found to be cheap and lively substitutes for choirs and incense. On the concourse, the clock could have stopped at 1901, but for Sir Robert Lorimer's anti-gothic memorial to those employees of the Glasgow & South Western Railway who had fallen in World War I. St Enoch symbolised another war – the Glasgow 'battle of the companies', a GSW 'victory' over the Caledonian.

In 1880 it was Scotland's premier passenger terminal, with an hotel to match. In 1950 it might be on crutches, but one thing it never lacked was mystery.

The complex was remarkable for the number of entrances. Off the passage parallel to Dunlop Street was a grimy underground booking office with stairs leading to all the platforms. From Maxwell Street a stairway got you right onto the concourse. In St Enoch Square a cluster of rather tatty shops and refreshment bars huddled beneath the gothic arches supporting a 1 in 13 terraced carriageway, with a central iron-and-glass gothic verandah having four doorways to the main booking hall. At the top of the terrace, vehicles used a muscular cast-iron portal. Hotel patrons (if they wished to avoid the trains or being classed as tradesmen) used a fussy little groined open porch at the foot of the gothic parade.

St Enoch was by far the gloomiest of the Glasgow terminal quartet. The train indicator looked like a rood screen in a church, while the monkish booking-office within praying distance of the carriageway gave the impression that it was designed for larger traffic which might come on the excommunication of the motor-car. The hydraulic hoists on the platforms were entombed in little corbelled wooden boxes which to the uninitiated might have been confessionals.

On the concourse a squalid railbar served as a refectory. For angels, there were pigeons and starlings who, ignoring the blast of engines and wire netting hung up beneath the edge of the roof, unsanctimoniously deposited their offerings on both believers and heretics. Communion (or rather the devil) was represented by the spirituous aroma of whisky from the bonded warehouses under the station.

from *Glasgow Stations*, Colin Johnston & John R. Hume, 1979

Only a couple of years after St Enoch Station opened, Glasgow suffered a financial scandal with the collapse of The City Bank. Fiction has given us a fine description of scenes outside the Bank's headquarters in Virginia Street, not far from the station:

Arthur asked her if she were going direct to his mother-in-law at Monteith Row – in which case she might accompany him by George's Square and the Candleriggs. But Phoebe thanked him and said that she had promised herself to go down Buchanan Street, then by Argyle Street and the Trongate, so that she might see what was showing in the autumn shop-windows. Arthur bade her a hasty goodbye and hurried off.

In Buchanan Street, too, there was an air of excitement. Phoebe, having been in the country so long, set about examining each window display with immense relish. But presently she found her attention caught by the excited voices of passers-by. The City Bank. Always the City Bank.

It was now long past nine. In front of the *Glasgow Herald* office there was a small crowd of people. She crossed over and asked a boy who looked like a young clerk what the crowd meant. They were trying to get further news of the City Bank. As she reached Argyle Street, morning passengers were pouring out of St Enoch's Square from the great, newly-built railway station. Urchins selling late editions of the morning papers were doing a roaring trade. She took her way along Argyle Street. Here in the rush of Glasgow's busiest street the excitement seemed swallowed up.

Phoebe was enjoying herself thoroughly now. She took each of the many windows in turn, gazing her fill. At last she decided to buy some small thing as an excuse for going inside to see the still greater wonders there.

She was turning to go back to the main entrance when she became conscious that people were hurrying along in excited knots on the other side of the street. For a moment she stood looking, and then, anxious to miss nothing, she picked up her skirts and ran over to see what it was all about. Presently she found herself at the corner of Virginia Street, a street which, in the ordinary way, was quiet, business-like, unobtrusive and without interest for a young girl.

Some little way up there was a large crowd of people standing. All of them were gazing up at a doorway. In a moment more she had joined them. She saw now that those about her were very excited, pressing forward, it seemed, towards this door. She craned her neck to see better and was able to read the words 'The City Bank of Glasgow, Head Office.'

She spoke to a woman by her side. 'Why is everybody waiting here?'

The woman, poorly dressed in black, turned. 'A don't ken whit everybody's waitin' for. A jist ken A'm waitin' till it's ten o' clock, to let me get ma money oot o' that place,' she said acidly.

A man in front of them looked round. 'You'll get no money oot o' that place.'

'Aye. A'll get it oot." The woman's voice broke hysterically. "It's either that, or gang to the puirshoose.'

'It's ten now,' the man said, and as he spoke a clock somewhere could be heard striking out ten strokes. The hour when, upon a normal day, all honourable banks threw open their doors and looked the world square in

THE STOPPAGE OF THE CITY OF GLASGOW BANK

The Mitchell Library

'Robbers! Thieves! Scoundrels!' Mayhem at the City Bank offices

the face. But this one it seemed could not. Voices became more high-pitched and excited. Women began to weep. The special staff of police, who had been sent against serious trouble, kept shouting not to block the street entirely. Their continual cry of 'Move on, please!' could be heard above the din. Here and there a sympathetic policeman could be seen telling a weeping woman to go home; that she was doing no good by standing here, that if she had City Bank notes in her possession she could turn them into coin elsewhere. From time to time people called out that they were ruined. They shouted the words 'Robbers! Thieves! Scoundrels!'

from *Wax Fruit*, Guy McCrone, 1947

Eventually, after its false-starts, the District Subway joined its bigger brother in St Enoch Square:

Operations have just been begun on the proposed Glasgow subways, which are to be worked by wire-cable haulage. Beginning at St. Enoch Square, the new line will cross under the Clyde at Dixon Street; then by Bridge Street and Scotland Street on the south side of the river it reaches Govan, where the river is re-crossed. The subway line then turns round by Partick and Byar's Road to reach the Great Western Road, which it keeps running underneath till Cowcaddens is reached. Finally, it returns by Buchanan Street to St. Enoch Square.

from *Strattens' Glasgow and its Environs*, 1891

But the construction was not achieved without difficulty:

ALARMING ACCIDENT IN SUBWAY:
Fire in the working under the Clyde:
13 men imprisoned for 12 hours.

A fire, by which the lives of 13 workmen were jeopardised for the long period of 12 hours, broke out last night in that portion of the works of the Glasgow District Subway between St Enoch Square and the south bank of the river at Carlton Place.

Within each tunnel is a lining of wood, while there is also a roadway of planks. Compressed air is driven into each chamber and carried to the face of the workings by means of a bogie or air-pipe, 2" in diameter, at a pressure of about 14lbs per sq. inch. The men, some of whom are miners, and others labourers, work in 8-hour shifts.

At about 8 o'clock last night the lockman who has charge of the entrance to the tunnel situated under St Enoch Square came running forward to the face of the workings and informed John White, foreman of the squad, that the timber of the lock had caught fire. The fire speedily assumed a most serious aspect, the tar-saturated wood and the pitch lining of the iron causing a heavy smoke.

Evening Times, 15 December 1894

The only means of rescue was to cut into the iron tunnel wall, which was separated from its twin by six feet of wet shifting sand. At 3 am, a hole was broken through, enabling fresh air to enter the smoke-filled chamber where the men were trapped. A bottle of brandy was passed through, and after five hours a large enough break was made in the wall to extricate the men.

Speaking to a representative of the *Evening Times* this morning one of the rescued men, pale and jaded with his long imprisonment underground, said:

'When we saw that we couldn't get out by the lock we lay down to die, and that's the fact. The pitch-pine packing and the tar on the iron plates made a stifling smoke. We lay with our faces close to the ground. Scarcely a word was spoken. We were nearly suffocated, but we kept the air-pipe playing in our midst, passing it from man to man.'

'I was richt gled to get a sook o' the fresh air, sir, through that wee pipe,' said another man. 'Gin it had failed we would a' hae been deid men lang ere this. The bottle o' brandy did us a hantle guid, but efter a' a bottle disna gang far among 13 men, does it?'

Evening Times, 15 December 1894

The fire was allowed to burn itself out. The cause was found to have been a dropped candle in the wood store; the resulting fire was intensified by the existence of tar linings on the ironwork. However, the lessons were not learned: a later fire at Govan killed two men.

The first day's operation on the Subway seemed to be a remarkable success, but late in the evening, there was a collision just outside St Enoch Station. The system was immediately closed, and did not re-open until five weeks later.

COLLISION ON THE SUBWAY

After one day's trial, in the course of which the Glasgow District Subway has been the scene of a breakdown, a collision and an accident to an employee, the line is closed today.

At St Enoch Station a placard bearing in large letters the words NO ADMITTANCE hangs on the gate. Beyond this no information is vouchsafed to the public or even to the representatives of the press as to why the line is closed or when it is likely to be reopened.

The rush of intending travellers yesterday was something extraordinary, and as the day advanced the various stations were besieged.

A perfect mania for subway travel seemed to seize the citizens and after darkness set in there was a crowd in front of each station doorway that fairly blocked the pavement. Downstairs the narrow platforms were filled, and as each car came forward there was a dangerous rush to gain admittance.

The opinion was freely expressed that people should not have been allowed to pass the turnstiles unless there was a reasonable possibility of carrying them to their destination.

The cars ran fairly well until half past three o' clock, when the cable slipped from one of the pulleys on the outer circle line between Cowcaddens and Buchanan Street stations. A car was approaching at the time, but the driver promptly slackened the grip, applied the brake, and stopped the car. No damage was done or any person injured, but the passengers had to scramble to the nearest station.

About five minutes to eleven o' clock an alarming collision, by which 19 persons were injured, fortunately none of them seriously, took place in the tunnel between 200-300 yards south from St Enoch Station.

It appears that car No 15, which was driven by John Ross, 175 James Street, Bridgeton, was standing on the line waiting for the signal to proceed to St Enoch Station. Just then, through some cause as yet unexplained, car No 5, in charge of George Henderson, 289 Parliamentary Road, came up behind. The impact, especially as it took place in the tunnel, greatly alarmed the passengers.

At the time of the accident the cable was said to be running at the rate of about 10 miles an hour, or two thirds of the maximum speed.

Notwithstanding these untoward events, many persons went to the stations this morning with the intention of travelling by the Subway, and seemed greatly disappointed when they found the gates closed.

Last night there was quite a scene at St Enoch Station. The public, in their anxiety to get down to platform, fairly took possession of the premises and bowled over the officials. Had the police not come to the rescue, there is no saying what might have happened. As it was the stationmaster was pitched onto the line and had a narrow escape in not coming in contact with the rope.

Evening Times, Tuesday 15 December, 1896

Despite the ill-omens of the opening day, the Glasgow District Subway was to prove a great success. One photograph taken in high summer at St Enoch Station shows two advertising posters extolling the virtues of the Subway as 'The Coolest and Quickest' means of travel in the city.

The Glasgow & South Western Railway's great St Enoch terminus saw its own disaster, on a much greater scale than that which marred the opening of the Subway, in the summer of 1903. A train arriving from Ardrossan crashed into the buffers and, although it was moving at only ten mph, sixteen people were killed.

The G&SWR's great new station and hotel were partly a result of the Company's close relationship with the Midland Railway, which was famed for its provision of lavish facilities. The St Enoch Hotel out-smarted even the hitherto un-matched Central Station Hotel.

For a time, there was great civic pride in the opulence and sophistication offered by the two great railway hotels, but by the thirties, there was a kind of discomfort with the idea of the extravagance, which was hardly available to everyone. It was clearly not hard during wartime to be aware of the incongruity:

Wednesday 5 March 1941

[Anna] is working at a canteen at the Central Station on Saturday nights; says there are always up to fifty boys who can't find anywhere to stay, asleep with their heads on the tables. One day thirty ship-wrecked seamen came from Greenock in the small hours, but the Central Hotel wouldn't take them in, not even to the lounge to sit down or have a wash – they were too dirty. At last the Beresford took them. She is furious, says there oughtn't to be two luxury hotels in Glasgow, either Central or St Enoch's, not both.

from *Among you taking Notes, the Wartime Diary of Naomi Mitchison, 1939–1945*, 1986

Numerous writers have, over the years, taken the opportunity to set scenes, not all of them celebrating the more pleasant sides of life, in the streets of the city centre. Within a stone's throw of what had been the 'solemn, dreamy' Square and the shops, businesses and coffee houses which attracted the early visitors were placed the drunks and the gangs of the twenties and thirties.

The Herald

St Enoch Square photographed before the Parish Church was demolished in 1926

For all practical purposes I now lived and worked in the slums of Winton. The change was alarming, the locality deadly. Back-to-back tenements surrounded us, interspersed with narrow streets and mean alleys in which one saw exhibited every sign and symptom of poverty and misery – the shawled women, idle men, and worst of all, the ragged, rickety, deformed children. Perpetually noisy, dirty and choked with traffic, Argyle Street seemed to me a running sore. Saturday night on its crowded flaring pavements was saturnalia: drunks rolling around, lying in the gutter, or being frog-marched to the police station, sailors on leave from the docks looking for trouble, factions of the rival football 'brake' clubs fighting it out with fists and knives after the match, while with a clash of cymbals, a thump of the drum and a blare of brass that heightened the pandemonium, the Salvation Army paraded up and down, pausing from time to time to sing a hymn, preach the terrors of damnation, and pass the tambourine.

from *A Song of Sixpence*, A J Cronin, 1964

Despite all the best endeavours of the city authorities, the poorer, squalid areas somehow managed to attract a large custom from society's discarded misfits and the many others who were simply not accepted elsewhere.

There is at least one public-house within a stonethrow of the Tron clock where the licence-holder, in order to lure customers, supplies beer and porter

The Mitchell Library

The New Subway *illustrated in* The Baillie *a few days before opening*

at a penny a glass. The quality of the liquor is guaranteed, and for a very small sum the denizens of this thickly-populated locality can purchase a few hours of oblivion. In this grog shop there is no sitting accommodation, and sometimes in the space in front of the bar there is a dead wall of human beings four deep, drinking, cursing, and indulging in the coarsest of ribald talk.

Not in the worst dens of New York can a more brutalised crowd be witnessed. Bareheaded and barefooted women with infants in their arms, uncouth Magdalenes scarred with the leprosy of sin, men on the borderland of delirium tremens, whose slumbers will be disturbed by weird spectral sights that will make the blood run cold in their veins are there, and no matter how intoxicated they are served without the least reluctance. . .

North British Daily Mail, 7 November, 1892

The purple prose of the tabloids was readily accepted and the tone set for the image of Glasgow's streets for the next three decades.

Razor King had marked all three of his enemies before the fight had lasted two minutes. Their bare fists were no defence against the terrible weapons. They could not even use their feet effectively in their wild efforts to guard their faces. They shouted and cursed and the blood flowed in streams.

The tumult was becoming dangerous and the policemen came running with drawn batons. Johnnie leapt into his last attack and embedded one razor in the face of a young man who collapsed in the doorway of the picture house. He slashed out with the other razor and then threw the weapon away and ran like a hare between a double line of stationary trams. The police were pounding at his feet, but he turned into Glassford Street well ahead of them and, running easily, soon out-distanced all pursuit, dropping into a walk at last in the Candleriggs.

He was unhurt and unmarked and almost bursting with exultation. For he had tackled three hooligans unaided and all three of them would have to go to the infirmary – stretcher cases he believed.

from *No Mean City*, Alexander McArthur and H Kingsley Long, 1935

A much more truthful, vibrant, picture of life in the city-centre streets is given by Archie Hind. His descriptions of people going about their daily routines in the late 1940s make them almost tangible, as he evokes sights, sounds and smells which have already been lost to us. His fish porters, '. . .their heads covered in snoods of hessian' seem almost three-dimensional:

When he got off the tram he walked down Stockwell Street towards the Clyde. The pavement was jammed with people and when he walked under the railway bridge he was forced at times to wait while the commercial lorries backed in from the street underneath the archways where the carriers' quarters were, and chandlers' stores and warehouses. There was a strong composite smell of oil and sugar, and as he walked further down the street, of fish. He turned to the left, walking through the street outside the fishmarket. At the angle between the pavement and the side of the buildings there was a miniscule of dried horse dung and fish scales. There were patches of wet on the tarmacadam of the road and scatterings of grain where an impatient horse had shaken its nose-bag, a terrific flurry and scatter of hooves as a carter backed his horse into an archway, his voice ringing out in authoritative yelps, 'Hup! Hup! Hup!' and the thudding of fish boxes as the porters lifted and dumped them, their heads covered in snoods of hessian. Mat walked on underneath the railway bridges, past the sordid street markets where all sorts of junk was sold, past the rag stores and the red brick city mortuary and the Police Courts.

He turned up past the gates of the Glasgow Green to the parapet of the bridge from where he could see the old Clyde, the colour of a back court puddle, winding in through the Green towards the centre of the city. Up Crown Street was a vista of dust and ashes. Mat had walked all this time with his head down, watching the toes of his shoes as they peeped in and out, in

Kelvingrove Art Gallery

"There was a strong composite smell of oil and sugar, and as he walked further down the street, of fish." A pencil and wash drawing by Muirhead Bone hauntingly complements Archie Hind's description

and out, from under the hem of his coat. Now as he stood on the bridge he felt the need for some sensuous stimulation, something which would destroy his grimy grey feeling of nothingness. Above the buildings the sky was harsh from a washy diffuse sunlight.

He was standing on the bridge looking over the parapet into the dirty water, at the very spot where Boswell had stood and looked at the widest streets in the whole of Europe. *Gles Chu!* The dear green place! Now a vehicle sclerosis, a congestion of activity! He felt for a cigarette in his pocket and the match which he lit flared bitterly in the cold air. The city about him seemed so real, the buildings, the bridge, the trams, the buses, so separate and hard and discrete and other.

He felt again a wave of nostalgia for another kind of existence – waxed fruit, sword sticks, snuff, tobacco, shining brass valves, steam pipes, jet ware, wag-at-the-wa's, horse-hair sofas, golf cleeks, cahootchie balls – all the symbols of confidence, possibility, energy, which had lived before this knotted, tight, seized-up reality which was around him had come to be.

from *The Dear Green Place*, Archie Hind, 1966

Many people will have memories of one famous St Enoch institution, round the corner in Howard Street:

Probably the larger proportion of fish merchandise comprehended in Glasgow's diurnal food supply is passed through the hands of the eminent fish purveying firm of Messrs Sawers. The opening of their present emporium at 11, 13 and 15 West Howard Street on 8 October 1890 was signalised by a large banquet, to which were invited many of the most influential merchants and tradesmen in the city.

The tessellated floor, the hand-painted tile panels of which the walls are composed, the appointments in marble and granite work, the beautiful sign which dignifies the front entrance, the oyster bar, and saloon at the rear, are all features of the establishment appropriate to its class of trade and also to its commercial distinction.

Messrs Sawers have done much to popularise Finnan haddocks and Loch Fyne herrings – two commodities in which the firm specially deal – as against the many imitations with which unprincipled traders have attempted to satiate the public demand.

No class of fish, poultry or game is excluded from their comprehensive operations, and Messrs Sawers are thus in a position to furnish with equal satisfaction the most common produce of sea or river and the much admired dainties of the epicure.

from an advertisement in *Strattens' Glasgow and its Environs*, 1891

Opposite: Candleriggs in 1955, showing 'a congestion of activity' which seems unfamiliar today

The Herald

'The appointments in marble and granite work' which characterised Sawers in Howard Street

And having purchased your 'dainties' you go for the bus . . .

My first week in the job and I'm on with a cunt who shall remain anonymous for the simple reason he's still in the garage. We gets to fucking Argyle Street – 3 o'clock on a Saturday afternoon and the place is mobbed man really mobbed; we stops at Jamaica Street traffic lights. I'd been late to get on the bus and it was so fucking busy I'd no even had a chance to see who was driving never mind the state he was in so anyway, the bus, stopped, for fucking ages, and all the punters're beginning to fidget and look about, but I'm so fucking new at the game I don't know anything's up – I'm rushing round getting the fares in quick, having a wee kind of inner competition to see if I can clear the top deck before the lights change or something.

I didn't even notice they'd been at green and back to red and back to fucking green again, till I starts hearing all the beep beeps, and then I looks out the window, and all the traffic, rows and rows, all jamming up, all beeping their horns and fucking

I know who it was.

What?

Who you're talking about, I know who it is.

Naw you dont.

Reilly snorted.

You dont.

Aye I fucking do.

I must've told you then.

How?

Cause you wouldnt fucking know unless, that's how.

Reilly shrugged and then he smiled. Okay, what happened?

Hh.

Naw, tell me.

What d'you mean tell me! if you already know what's the fucking point.

Reilly shrugged.

Hines swivelled on the seat and raised his boots onto the back of the seat in front; he closed his eyelids.

from *The Busconductor Hines*, James Kelman, 1984

The final ignominy for the grand St Enoch Station and Hotel was demolition. In fact, their demolition was the means of destruction of another city asset: thousands of tons of stone from both buildings was used to infill Queens Dock at Finnieston. Railway station and dock both, depressingly, became car parks.

Having done what was necessary, Minty was slow climbing the steps of the Underground and as he came out into St Enoch's Square, he rested a minute before tackling the curving hill that led to the pedestrians' entrance to the car park.

The morality of what he had done wasn't his concern. All it meant to him was something troublesome and tiring, but worth it.

St Enoch's Station had been a part of the Glasgow he knew. Now the high, arched, glass roof that had fascinated him as a boy was patched with sky. What had seemed before unimaginably far away now only served to give perspective to the vastness of the distance beyond it. Those squares of starlit sky were a bottomlessness he was falling into. There were acres of macadam where the rails had been – nowhere for him to go from here.

Walking among the pillars, he could see no light or movement among the cars. Then far out beyond the roof, he saw the lights of a car flash on and off. As he walked towards it, the front passenger door swung open.

from *Laidlaw*, William McIlvanney, 1977

The disrepair and neglect which had overtaken the Glasgow & South Western Railways station also eventually afflicted the Subway, whose eccentric fortress in St Enoch Square had become something of a symbol.

The ticket office in St Enoch Square was housed in what can only be called a miniature Rhineland castle, but the fantasy was soon over, for after some narrow grimy stairs you were on an island platform standing before a 'Q-Here' sign painted in white on the ancient concrete paving. Suddenly a train crawled in, a diminutive red affair, but only when you were on the move did you know why it had to crawl. While the conductor guard punched your tickets (at the end of the journey he collected them and deposited them in the box under the wooden stool in his compartment) cracked mahogany panels vibrated beneath a lining of formica and windows visibly moved in their frames.

It was a miracle how this 1896 rolling stock held together, and the true connoisseur (if not choking to death in a smoking compartment, though the line was never steam-hauled) could spot a 1930 light bulb holder, a 1920 match striker, a 1950 chrome handle, and if he was lucky, a Victorian brass one.

from *Glasgow Stations*, Colin Johnston & John R Hume, 1979

Much has been made over the years, in fact and fiction, of Glasgow's pubs. The tradition began with 18th century coffee-houses, and continued in the 19th with chop-houses and a variety of popular restaurants. Of course, the fiction of the razor-gangs also gave us the vilest of drinking dens, but many of the city's pubs, real and imagined, where the genteel art of elbow-lifting is practised, deserve to be remembered with pleasure.

To dine well at a moderate cost is an art not to be taught in books, albeit much has been written on the subject. Two men may enter a restaurant where the cooking is unexceptionable and the service perfect, and order their dinners. It is not unlikely that the one will dine badly off a villainous selection of viands, each perfect in its way, while the other will dine well at half the cost, from his superior taste and knowledge of the gastronomic art. All that can be done in this work is to indicate the places where a man may dine well if he knows how, and to advise the man who does not know how to order his own dinner to betake himself to one of the hotels where a good table-d'hote dinner is to be had at a moderate cost. Very excellent dinners, of three or four courses, served in first-class style in the best restaurants, can be had from 2s to 3s 6d, exclusive of liquors. The favourite grill-room is that of the Central Station Hotel (entrances from Hope Street, and the arrival platform in the Station), but in all the principal dining-rooms, such as the St Enoch's – one of the largest and best in the city – steaks and chops from the grill are to be had. The principal restaurants near the centre of the city are Brown's, 195 St Vincent Street; Ferguson and Forrester's, 36 Buchanan Street; Stark's, 41 Queen Street; Thornton's, 108 Buchanan Street; and Watson and Blane's, 91 West George Street.

The man who does not belong to a club, and who wishes to give a dinner-party at a restaurant, and have it served in a private room, must first consult his means. If the cost is not to be considered, a dinner perfect in every appointment, from the wines down to the souvenir menu, may be had at many of the above.

from *Kirkwood's Dictionary of Glasgow*, 1884

J J Bell made the interesting observation that there were relatively more people about in Glasgow late at night in the eighties and nineties than in the 1920s. Many banquets, dinners, balls and smoking concerts were held in the large new hotels and in the Waterloo Rooms during these late Victorian decades, and the magnificent Grosvenor Restaurant with its marble staircase, was being built to cater specially for social functions.

Most of the restaurants were still in the Argyle Street district, although the Bridgegate, where the first eating-houses had been established early in the century, was no longer in favour. But MacArthur's, with its red plush cubicles, automatic music and sixpenny ashet pies was in the Trongate, not far away, and so were Scott's and the Bank in Queen Street, Sloan's in the Argyle Arcade, Pie Smith's in Maxwell Street, the Silver Grill near the Argyle Street-Jamaica Street crossing – 'where the French Renaissance began in Glasgow' – His Lordship's Larder in St Enoch Square, F and F's and the Queen's in Buchanan Street, and the Corn Exchange in Gordon Street. These and various chop-houses, such as Joseph White's in Gordon Street and the City Commercial in Union Street, maintained many of the old traditions, such as serving sheep's head and pig's trotters on Wednesdays, and put in their windows such delectables as cooked sirloins of beef, lobsters and tubs of oysters.

The Eagle Vaults, the Bodega and the American Bar in Jamaica Street were all much used in the nineties. The American Bar was conducted in proper style. It was where 'you got the bottle of Bourbon rye put down for you to help yourself, and pecked ad lib at cloves, olives, cinnamon bark and crackers.'

from *The Second City*, by C A Oakley, 1967

Pub. . . wine bar. . . bistro. . . disco – things change. . .

Lorries rattled over the cobbles in West Nile Street with the same tearing scream as of yore; newsboys shouted; clerks hurried in from the suburbs to extension classes, or to billiards. He turned back along Gordon Street. The newspaper shop in the flagged way leading from Buchanan Street to Queen Street still showed the illustrated weeklies on strings in its window. So did the stationer's shop farther on, on the north side of the Royal Exchange, whither he walked – just to see. That suggested the 'Papeleria,' and he must needs go down to St Enoch Square – to discover if it still existed. There was a slight change there; one entered it on the street level instead of going down steps to it, and Deadwood Dick and Jack Harkaway and Ching Ching had disappeared. The newcomers might appeal to the youth of today – Martin could not say, no longer a youth of the day.

from *Justice of the Peace*, Frederick Niven, 1914

T & R Annan & Sons Ltd

The junction of of Argyle Street and Jamaica Street in the days of horse-drawn carts and trams

A buzzing of blood went into Will's ears. Never in his life had he been assailed by the pathetic in this frightening way. In comparison, Bill Bailey and his listeners were he-men.

'Want another?' Joe asked.

'One minute,' said Will and he looked around.

'Where's the lavatory?' he asked the barman.

'Through that way.'

Will edged his way through, was involuntarily stopped by his nostrils on the threshold, held his breath, and went into the latrine. Men's backs and shoulders; one or two swaying in their drink. The fellow next to him was leaning forward, supported by the forehead which pressed against the flag-stone wall. All at once the horizontal pipe a few inches above the man's head noisily gushed out water through its small perforations.

The water descended upon his cap, soaked it, and trickled down his face. His whole body convulsed and his mouth ejected a violent gush of vomit, which hit the flagstone and spat back upon Will's clothes. Will let out a harsh grunt of disgust and began wildly brushing the stuff off with his naked hand.

Slowly the face twisted round at him. Black burning eyes. The eyes held him, torture drawn to fine points. The face drew back from the wall, slowly, and steadied, concentrating on Will in a demoniacal satire and hatred. Only as the body squared up did Will notice that the right arm was missing.

from *Wild Geese Overhead*, Neil Gunn, 1939

The dreaded Glasgow Saturday became something of a nightmare. Patterns of work – and pay – allowed no weekday recklessness. For untold thousands, Saturday was a miasma of two routine obsessions:

On Saturday night Argyle Street holds Saturnalia – not the 'Continental Saturnalia' we hear so much about, but a time of squalid license, when men stagger out of shuttered public-houses as out of a pit, and the street echoes to insane roaring and squabbles, to the nerve collapse that ends a day's debauch of drink and football.

from *Glasgow in 1901*, by J H Muir, 1901

Thankfully, matters improved beyond belief, and Glasgow eventually had pubs of familiar character and drinkable beer which, before the advent of the horrors of someone else's choice of over-loud music, encouraged the twin arts of conversation and elbow-lifting. Everyone should have a 'Duffy's':

True to his weekly habit, and as befitted a typical tenement husband, Peter Kerr, the while that Annie was counting the halfpennies and pennies of her week-end purchases and the children amusing themselves with difficulty at home, might have been found, one of a crowd similarly inclined, rubbing aggressive shoulders to retain his position at the counter of Duffy's bar situated under the bridge at Argyle Street.

The saloon was severely taxed to accommodate its usual Saturday evening patrons. . . argumentative football enthusiasts direct from the match; quiet prolific whisky drinkers of the deeply-rooted craving; irresponsible youths giving scope to a misguided impression of the requirements of manhood; cheerful casuals anxious to share their own good humour and another's benefice; regular patrons distinguished by their confident hand-waves and immediate responses; and a few sorrowful specimens of humanity just lounging around, hungry eyes following the lift of elbows.

All types and classes jostling, jumbling, loudly talking. Loudly venturing opinions in the raw accent of their town. Drinking and talking. Drinking to talk. . . to argue. . . to fight. A bedlam in miniature.

Duffy's bar quite merited the tremendous popularity it had gained as a rendezvous and debating ground. The bright lights glinted pleasantly on the array of whisky and liqueur bottles on the mirrored shelves behind the broad counter. The clink of glasses and the tinkle of cash register bell, rising above the hum of conversation and punctuating outbursts of ribald laughter, was pleasant music.

The long oval counter, the curtained alcoves lining the sides, the quality of the prints and watercolours on the varnished panels above these sitting-rooms, gave it a distinctive rich comfort not to be found in the ordinary run of public-houses. And, not the least distinctive feature of the establishment, Duffy himself, his rosy features and merry eyes radiating a welcome to everybody but the undesirables, in his counter stance just opposite the ever-moving swing-doors.

The Herald

The interior of Samuel Dow's pub in Mitchell Street, a well-known haunt of journalists

'See you at Duffy's.' The phrase has been repeated so often, has been over-heard so often, that it has become almost an unconscious habit to remark it. It is heard in every district. It is as well-known to the mansions as it is to the closes and the alleys. Sailors have carried its fame to the ends of the world.

Men drop into Duffy's with an easy familiarity who have never seen the inside of any other bar, who would scorn the idea of entering any other bar. Duffy's saloon is an institution. . . just as well-known, for instance, as Sawer's fish shop in Howard Street, or as the willow-pattern design of Low's confectionery containers. Their apology for drinking. A very good reason for an occasional lapse. An occasional lapse at least once each week. Under other circumstances they might concede that drinking was a sin. But here it becomes a very proper and respectable proceeding. Elbow-lifting, Glasgow's Saturday night occupation, takes on a genteel veneer when it is performed in Duffy's saloon.

from *Tenement*, John Cockburn, 1925

Just along from St Enoch Square lies the famous quayside of the Broomielaw – 'a grassy slope with broom growing on it'. A working quayside since a weigh-house and crane were built in 1662, the Broomielaw, and the steamers that went with it, have always retained a special resonance for Glaswegians.

The Broomielaw has not borne a broom 'cow' for many a year. 'Ane little quay' has gradually extended to a long line of wharves, where traffic reigns. Warehouses abound with goods from the four quarters of the globe, shops with a seafaring flavour, though the sea is not at hand, and they deal in the common necessaries of shore life; the homely dwellings of these humbler shop-keepers, sailors' lodging-houses, commercial hotels, look down upon the busy thoroughfare and the river highway.

Among the crowd of shipping, steamboats, multiplied mightily since Henry Bell's little *Comet* plied between Glasgow and Greenock, and was the wonder of the day – arrive at all hours at the Broomielaw. Many of them are Highland boats from 'Glasgow down the water,' the villa settlements that fringe the Clyde and the lochs. And far beyond the islands that begin with Bute and Arran is a Scotch archipelago – shaggy, heathery rocky, castle-crowned here and there, guarded by savage mountains and wild sounds. That is the region of green Morven near thunder-haunted Knapdale, pillared Staffa, sacred Iona, lonely Barra and Canna, and the primitive, desolate Western Hebrides, in which Stornoway ranks as a big town.

from *St Mungo's City*, Sarah Tytler, 1885

The train had moved out of the station, but just then it slowed down and stopped on the high bridge which there spans the Clyde. Joanna, from learning how many times a sovereign beat finely out would engirdle the earth,

Embarking at The Broomielaw *a fine photograph of about 1880 by George Washington Wilson in which the eye is nicely led past the steamers and sheds to the street activity behind*

looked up and out of the window. Below her, framed in the great transverse shanks of the iron grille, the water looked so beautiful that she could have called out. Yet something kept her quite still and mute in her corner.

It had been raining half an hour before, but now the sun gleamed on the brown surface of the river and on the wet, grey granite balustrades of the Jamaica Bridge. The bright red and yellow horse-cars flashed as they followed each other northwards and southwards along shining rails, and the passing craft on the water moved in a dun-coloured glory. By one bank some paddle-steamers were being repainted for the coming season. Joanna with the others had often sailed in them for summer cruises, and she knew by the number of funnels and their colours to which line each boat belonged. She knew the dredgers too, obstinate in mid-stream, with their travelling lines of buckets trawling glittering filth from the river-bed, while passing them, a string of half-submerged barges and rafts hung behind a little panting tug. Less familiar was a giant liner that made her slow way seaward. Her decks were deserted. Only a negro leaned, gazing, upon a rail astern.

This picture, cut into sections and made brilliant by the interposing trellis of black metal, appealed not so much to the little girl's untrained eye, as symbolically through her eye to her heart which leapt in response. The sunshine on that outgoing vessel and the great, glistening current of brown water filled her with painful yet exquisite longings. She did not know what ailed her, nor what she desired.

from *Open the Door*, Catherine Carswell, 1920

Now, with virtually all the shipping activity ceased, the picture is more dismal. The life brought to the river by paddle-steamers, the little 'cluthas', dredgers and cross-river ferries seems now to have come to an end too suddenly, without our noticing. By stealth. Like a theft. Glasgow needs to re-invent the River Clyde.

We climbed the circling ramp that led to the bridge over the Clyde. Across pouring ranks of cars I saw dock cranes and a glitter of light from the big river.

'If you went into that water,' Brond said, 'jumped, pushed or driven off the edge in a car, first requirement when they fished you out – if they fished you out – would be a stomach pump. Look there!' I caught a glimpse of a racing boat, young men pulling back on the oars. 'Jolly boating weather! When they lift it out the hull will be plastered with swabs of used toilet paper.'

from *Brond*, Frederic Lindsay, 1983

Taking the search for inspiration more seriously than most, the author of the following poem apparently wrote it while perched on a buoy on the River.

ODE TO THE CLYDE

Hail, great black-bosomed mother of our city,
Whose odoriferous breath offends the earth,
Whose cats and puppy dogs excite our pity,
As they sail past with aldermanic girth!
No salmon hast thou in thy jet-black waters,
Save what is adhering to the tins.
Thus thy adorers – Govan's lovely daughters –
Adorn thy shrine with offerings for their sins.
No sedges check thy flow, nor water lily;

Thy banks are unadorned with hip or haw,
'Cos why? – now, don't pretend you're *really* silly,
There ain't no lillies at the Broomielaw.
MacBrayne defiles thy face with coaly sweepings,
Into thy lap the tar expectorates;
The *Caledonia*'s cook his galley heapings
Casts in thy face as if at one he hates.

Yet thou art great. Though strangers hold their noses
When sailing down to Rothesay at the Fair,
The exiled sons would barter tons of roses
To scent thy sweetness on the desert air.

Charles J Kirk, 1910

An anonymous postcard view of steamers leaving Bridge Wharf

The paddle steamer *Caledonia* bulged fat and weighed low down with people. Yet more and more Glaswegians were queuing up at Bridge Wharf across from the Broomielaw and crushing merrily on to swell its sides fatter and fatter.

The hot sun sparkled the vivid kaleidoscope of coloured clothes and polished brass and dazzling paint.

Already the singing had started and men were chugging bottles of whisky from jacket pockets and women were chattering and laughing and children were dashing about getting lost.

A couple of middle-aged women, their fat bouncing and wobbly before them, were facing each other up for a dance, whacking their hands, galloping towards each other, pouncing on each other's arms, and uttering hair-raising 'heughs' as they birled each other round, spinning faster and faster, with everybody watching, singing and shouting, clapping hands and stamping feet.

At last the gang-planks were lifted, ropes flung aboard. The steamer gave a warning hoot and with much creaking, groaning and splashing, the *Caledonia's* paddles were set in motion, slowly at first, the water foaming and frothing; then gradually as it rocked away from Bridge Wharf, just by the George V Bridge, the paddles quickened and found their joyous rhythm and water-churning strength.

A band began to play in the centre of the middle deck. It consisted of four men in navy-blue suits and caps. One man strummed the banjo, another had a white hanky spread over his shoulder on which rested his fiddle and his head. Another energetically squeezed and pulled at a concertina and the fourth thumped with great concentration on an ancient piano.

Melvin, Catriona and Fergus sat for'ard on the top deck because there they could get all the sunshine and fresh air that was going. They also got quite a breeze and Catriona's long hair swirled and twirled and flowed out behind her.

'Make sure you enjoy every minute of this,' Melvin warned. 'It's costing me a pretty penny!'

from *The Breadmakers*, Margaret Thomson Davis, 1972

Having already met the crew of *The Maggie* in too-close proximity to the Subway, there is one opportunity to encounter those other favourite seamen, the crew of *The Vital Spark*. Neil Munro gave the intrepid Hurricane Jack at least one, entirely circular, trip on the Subway:

' "There's a lot o' fun I used to think I would indulge in if I had the money," said Hurricane Jeck, "and now I have the opportunity if I only had a friend like yoursel' to see me doin' it. I'm goin' to spend it aal in trevellin'." '

'And him a sailor!' commented the astonished Sunny Jim.

'He wass meanin' trevellin' on shore,' said Para Handy. 'Trains, and tramway cars, and things like that, and he had a brulliant notion. It wass aye a grief to Jeck that there wass so many things ashore you darena do withoot a prosecution. "The land o' the Free!" he would say, "and ye canna take a tack on a train the length o' Paisley withoot a bit of a pasteboard ticket!" He put in the rest of that day I speak of trevellin' the Underground till he wass dizzy and every other hour he had an altercation wi' the railway folk aboot his ticket. "Take it oot o' that," he would tell them, handin' them a pound or two, and he quite upset the traffic. On the next day he got a Gladstone bag, filled it with empty bottles, and took the train to Greenock.

' "Don't throw bottles oot at the windows," it says in the railway cairrages; Jeck opened the windows and slipped oot a bottle or two at every quarter mile, till the Caledonian system looked like the mornin' efter a Good Templars' trip. They catched him doin' it at Pollokshields.

' "What's the damage?" he asked them, hanging' his arm on the inside strap o' a first-cless cairrage and smokin' a fine cigar. You never saw a fellow that could be more genteel.

' "It might be a pound a bottle," said the railway people; "we have the law for it."

' "Any reduction on takin' a quantity?" said Jeck. "I'm havin' the time o' my life; it's most refreshin'".'

from *The Complete Gentleman: Para Handy*, Neil Munro, 1931

GOVAN CROSS
IBROX
CESSNOCK
KINNING PARK
SHIELDS ROAD
WEST STREET
BRIDGE STREET
ST ENOCH

(**BUCHANAN STREET**)

COWCADDENS
ST GEORGE'S CROSS
KELVINBRIDGE
HILLHEAD
KELVIN HALL
PARTICK

For: Tourist Information Centre; Buchanan Street Bus Station; Queen Street Station; Old Athenaeum Theatre; Royal Concert Hall; Hutcheson's Hall; Trades House; City Chambers; Stock Exchange; Gallery of Modern Art; George Square; College of Building & Printing; College of Commerce; College of Food Technology; City Campus, Glasgow Caledonian University; Strathclyde University

ANDREW BUCHANAN, of the 'American Merchants' Buchanan, Hastie and Company (tobacco importers) owned much of the ground between St Enoch Square and Gordon Street. In 1777, he decided to expand his domain:

> A street to be opened directly opposite St Enoch's Square.
>
> Andrew Buchanan Esq merchant, proposes to enlarge his entry in Argyle Street, opposite to St Enoch's Square, to 40 feet, free of every incumberance, such as stairs or other projections. This entry will lead into a street running to the northward, opening equally on each side, so as to make a street of 70 feet in breadth. The ground abounds in fine pit water in digging 10 or 12 feet. Access also may be had at small expense to good running water (viz St Enoch's Burn). It is proposed that purchasers should subject themselves to some regulations for the ornament of the street. For sight of the ground and plan of the street, please apply to the proprietor.
>
> from *The Glasgow Journal*, 3 April 1777

From its beginning, it was clear that the new street was going to be rather grand and showy:

90

Buchanan Street, the Regent Street of the Western Metropolis. Its history begins in 1778, and was named after the landlord. The advertisements of the day describe the situation as 'rural and agreeable'. Agreeable it still may be, but rural it certainly is no longer. The shops are the gayest, and the locality is the most attractive to the pedestrian of any in the town. At the upper end of the street, approached by rather a steep incline, is the old terminus of the Caledonian Railway, used chiefly for north and local trains. The Western Club, by the same architect (Hamilton), who designed the Royal Exchange, is a chaste and handsome building, admirable for its purpose. In St Vincent Place are the handsome offices of the Clydesdale Bank (by Burnet). The Stock Exchange, in Buchanan Street again, is a fine specimen of Venetian and Gothic blended with an eye to the purposes of daily life. Many people stop to have a peep at the wonderful Machine Room of the *Glasgow Herald* and *Evening Times*. The building itself is most sumptuous, and is a striking feature of this fine street. At the southern end of it the shops rival those of Paris and London.

from *Strattens' Glasgow and its Environs*, 1891

A period of remarkably flourishing trade followed in Glasgow. The recent prosperous years had all been leading up to this flush of enterprise and attainment. The expansion, if it did not pervade every source, reached to many departments of trade. Never had the hammers of the boiler-makers and the ship-builders rung with more inspiring din, sending sonorous music down the misty river. Never had such strings of casks rumbled in and out of the sugar warehouses and the spirit vaults. Never had St Rollax and its sister chimneys vomited forth heavier volumes of tainted smoke. Never had the Exchange been so thronged and so busy, or Buchanan Street so crowded with promenaders and purchasers, or the Broomielaw so besieged with the shipping of all nations.

Mechanics and mill-hands had the maximum of wages. The homes of employers abounded not only in comforts, but in expensive, inappropriate luxuries – in port wine, oysters, and early strawberries; in rosewood couches, pianos, and feather-beds. The women of the class figured, on high days and holidays, in silk and lace. The custom of the smaller shops became steady and richly remunerative; that of the larger swelled enormously, till it reached so grand a scale of fortune-making that it ceased to be worth while asking the hitherto crucial question whether the process was wholesale or retail.

Even the people who were least touched by the strong impetus, awoke to a distant rumour of the city's tremendous transactions and mighty profits, and invented fables more incredible still of the men who were puddlers, or winders, or dock-labourers today and princes tomorrow; of granite palaces which were equivalent to streets paved with gold. The risings in life at the Australian and American diggings were a trifle to the upheavals in Glasgow society – nothing was said at this moment of the corresponding downfalls. The gold nuggets of Ballarat and San Francisco were not to be spoken of in a breath with the floating capital of Glasgow – the real nuggets were bills of lading and invoices. Tyre and Ormus, in their traditions, must thenceforth hide their diminished heads; Manchester bolstered up by Salford, and Liverpool backed by Birkenhead, had better withdraw from the idle competition.

from *St Mungo's City*, Sarah Tytler, 1885

Buchanan Street had direct access to the four Glasgow railway terminals. St Enoch, Central Station (opened in 1897 to replace the original Bridge Street Station), Queen Street (opened in 1842 to handle traffic to Edinburgh) and Buchanan Street Station, opened in 1849 for routes to the far north. All four were loved for themselves, although they were entirely different in character.

From the Post Office steps you see Queen Street Station rise like a great yellow half-moon, and within is cheery comfort, very welcome after snow or rain. Nice brown trains are setting off to England, others,less pleasant to look at, start for more fascinating destinations – Fife, Inverness, romantic spots in Scotland. At such a moment one loses the sense (heavy enough at other times) that Glasgow is a place cut off by its smoke and grime from the Scotland that foreigners think of when they figure us standing in kilts upon hills 'quite inaccessible' – Scott's 'land of brown heath and shaggy wood.' It is not for nothing that the railway has headquarters in Edinburgh and goes by the Waverley route. It is the most romantic station in Glasgow, and we can forgive its trains for being irregular, since they take us in the end to pleasant places.

Buchanan Street Station is more ancient, but its romance is of the embalmed, petrified, museum-like kind. And Queen Street is not romantic simply, but also agricultural. Something in the dear, old, comfortable, unpretentious look of it tells you as much. It is more like a tavern – a battered caravanserai – than a station, its waiting-room quite like an inn-parlour, with space for four tolerably stout farmers, and a dark polished, mahogany table. There is passage, too, for a porter should he wish to bring coals, but he never does, and so the illusion of the inn-parlour is maintained. Out on the platform there is a spring of water, at which Ne'er Day people will mix their drink. What with whisky and fruit and newspapers, it provides more than any other place in the city for tired holiday-makers from the country. On feein' days the smell in it is richly of the soil, and many little scenes of yokel fun are enacted there, like the more decent passages in Teniers' pictures. On market days the farmers may be traced from McColl's (where they have ended with apple dumpling) to the station by the hay-seed and corn samples fallen from their pockets.

from *Glasgow in 1901*, J H Muir, 1901

Kelvingrove Art Gallery

A battered caravanserai – *an atmospheric pencil drawing of 'Queen Street Station' in 1910 by Muirhead Bone*

But Buchanan Street Station became very run-down, and affection for it soon waned:

Of all the ugly blots upon the Glasgow landscape Buchanan Street Railway Station stands easily first. It's an architectural abortion that would raise gall in the heart of an Eskimo; a chemical works or a charnel house is cheerful by comparison. Tenth rate suburban villages have gorgeous buildings erected for the reception of railway travellers; one of the most important railway termini in the greatest municipality on earth is a structure that an Irish pig-keeper would blush to keep his porkers in.

from *Glasgow Stations*, Colin Johnston and John R Hume, 1979

And it had obviously not been a great joy to work there. . .

Discipline was strict. D B Hanna, who obtained a clerkship at the Caledonian goods station at Buchanan Street, Glasgow, in 1875, recalled:
'The first thing I learned there was that Presbyterian strictness was nothing compared to one brand of railway rigidity. The office was six miles from home, and a few minutes walk from the South Side passenger station. The first morning train arrived there at nine o'clock. Wishing still to live at home, I asked my immediate superior to excuse me from beginning work until shortly after nine, if I made up the time at noon, or in the evening. He refused; and so, for a year I walked the six miles from Thornliebank six mornings a week.'

from *Trains of Recollection*, D B Hanna, Toronto, 1924

(quoted in *The Railway Station, a Social History*, J Richards and J MacKenzie, 1986)

Glasgow Central had everything, in particular an architect who ensured that it was a superbly designed space for the movement of crowds of people. Not quite so grand today perhaps, but still 'a contender'.

Cameron, in twenty years, since he had left St Mungo, had never returned to it even on the shortest visit. He spoke of it now with a sentimental air, and expressed a firm intention to go down and see the gaieties of July.

'I'll see a lot o' changes on Gleska,' he said. 'Twenty years! It looks like a lifetime! What would you say yoursel', Mr. Swan, was changed the most in Gleska in twenty years?'

Jimmy puckered up his brows and chewed a pencil, lost in thought.

'Well,' said he, 'there's the picture-palaces. where ye can get everything now except a dram and a bed for the night – they'll be new to ye. And then there's the Central Station; ye've never seen the Central since they altered it, have ye?'

'No,' said Cameron sadly. 'What's it like noo?'

'Oh, it's beyond words!' said Jimmy, rolling ribbons up. 'Ye could put the whole o' the folk in Perth between the bookstalls, and they would just look like a fitba' team. It's got the biggest, brawest, nameliest lavatory in Europe, doon a stair, where ye can get your hair cut, and a bath for sixpence. Lots o' men go down for baths and barberin', stayin' down for hours if they think their wives are lookin' for them.'

from 'Raising the Wind'– *Erchie & Jimmy Swan*, Neil Munro, 1993

A memory of that lavatory lingers as an enamelled sign bearing the silhouette of a hand with a pointing finger, and the legend 'Men's Lavvies.' underneath. The full stop after 'Lavvies' was clearly intended to assure readers that there was a lack of space on the sign rather than a wish to be sloppy with the language.

Strathkelvin District Libraries (MacEwan Collection)

A ubiquitous photograph of Central Station under siege

The site of Central Station had been the location of Glasgow's first theatre. Indeed, all the city's early theatres were close to the sites of the main railway stations, and all had a history of misfortune and disaster:

The first theatre in Glasgow was a temporary booth, fitted up in 1752, in the ruins of the archbishop's palace or castle, but was superseded in 1762 by a regular theatre erected in the district then known as Grahamstown. It stood on ground now occupied by the Central Railway Station, and was opened in 1764 by a company which included Mrs Bellamy. It seemed doomed to misfortune, for on the opening night it was much damaged by fire, and after a career of varied but generally indifferent success it was burned to the ground in 1782, when the whole wardrobe and properties, valued at £1,000, were destroyed. The next theatre, built in 1785, was in Dunlop Street, and was opened by a company that included Mrs Siddons, Mrs Jordan, and other distinguished performers. In the beginning of the following century it was found too small, and a new one was erected, partly by subscription, on the W side of Queen Street at a cost of £18,500. It was one of the largest and most elegant theatres then in Great Britain, but it was destroyed by fire in 1829. The Dunlop Street Theatre, which had been rebuilt in 1839-40, was now a building of showy but tasteless exterior, with statues of Shakespeare, Garrick, and Mr Alexander. In 1849, during a panic caused by a false alarm of fire, a rush for the doors caused the death of 65 people, and injury to a great many more. It was destroyed by fire in 1863, but underwent such repair as rendered it still the principal theatre in the city; but it had to be finally relinquished in 1868, in consequence of the operations of the Union Railway Company.

from *Groome's Ordnance Gazetteer*, 1893-95

When the Subway Station was opened at No 174 Buchanan Street, it had to burrow under the low-level lines of the nearby Queen Street Station of the Edinburgh and Glasgow Railway. The new station was forty feet below street level, making it the deepest on the system.

Buchanan Street, while a focus for grand shopping, was also an area of commerce of all varieties:

Tommy went upon his authorised way, along Argyle Street and into the great retail house to which the letter he carried was addressed. In the vestibule he was observed and recognised – to his great content – by the lordly man who stood there, was granted a little nod from him. Chucking his chest, he continued past the hum and buzz where ladies sat upon high-backed chairs with right-hand gloves drawn off, feeling the quality of the ends of bolts of cloth spread loose before them. He pattered up broad stairs, down which came other ladies, marched on upon the upper floor where were more counters and more ladies, these examining silks and satins, went on to a room of glass into which, on aerial wires, buzzed cash-containers like oranges, and there he handed his letter to a venerable gentleman within who, lowering his head, looked at him over the top of pince-nez, saying paternally the one word:

'Simson's?'

'Yes, sir.'

from *The Staff at Simsons*, Frederick Niven, 1937

A review of some of the great mercantile houses of Glasgow demonstrates the fact that the greatness of the city depends not upon an isolated industry, but upon a congeries of magnificent commercial enterprises, each carried out on a scale of magnitude quite unparalleled in the annals of modern industry. In this connection a pre-eminent rank must be assigned to the world-renowned establishment conducted under the style of Messrs Stewart and MacDonald . . . [of Buchanan Street, Argyle Street, Mitchell Street, and also London, Edinburgh, Birmingham, Hull, Leeds, Liverpool, Newcastle, Preston, Rochdale, Belfast, Dublin, Dunedin, Toronto, Montreal, Melbourne, Sydney, and Port Elizabeth!].

The warehouse embraces no fewer than thirty-four distinct departments of general wholesale drapery and fabrics, comprising the following features: cloths, silks, cottons, flannels, linens, ribbons, merinoes, prints, muslins, laces, hand-kerchiefs, haberdashery,yarns, winceys, carpets, tweeds, skirtings, wool shawls, fancy dresses, straw hats, millinery, flowers, white cottons, gloves, shirts, ready-made clothing, Bradford stuffs, stationery, and under-clothing.

Each department is under the most capable supervision, and so great are the firm's facilities and resources that the largest orders can be executed on the shortest notice, and in a manner reflecting the highest credit upon those responsible for the carrying-out of the executive functions.

The vast warehouses in Buchanan Street, Argyle Street and Mitchell Street contain an aggregate value of fully half a million, every item having been selected with the greatest care and judgement. Dress materials form a conspicuous feature in the turnover of the house. In this connection there are four distinct departments. English, French, German, and Scotch dress goods are held in endless variety, and Messrs Stewart and MacDonald export these fabrics to all parts of the globe.

advertisement from *Strattens Glasgow and its Environs*, 1891

Stewart and MacDonald was taken over in the 1950s by Frasers, along with their rivals Wylie & Lochead. The part of Fraser's existing building at 21-31 Buchanan Street was Stewart and MacDonalds' main warehouse.

Fiction closely mirrored the reality of such huge warehouses:

Entering Simson's one advanced along a corridor at the end of which, to left, was a door labelled *Office*. Ahead was another, a swing door, reinforced at its base with a sheet of zinc, so that it could be kicked open by men carrying loads and with no free hand. Its upper part was of frosted glass, save for a disc left transparent in the centre, like a bull's eye, toward the avoidance of collisions there. Swinging that open, most of the warehouse was revealed in one comprehensive glance.

The Shirtings department, of course, was not visible. You had to turn to right, and to right again, to enter it, but otherwise the main warehouse was clear to view between stacks of cloth of many sorts, columns of winceys, flannelette and the rest, that seemed flimsily to aid the red-painted iron columns in sustaining the roof. Upon that floor stood a long counter (of the Fancy Goods department) with a gap for further progress at either end. At that counter, Mr Maxwell, Corbett, and Johnny Leng, over their pattern and order-books, would look up without raising their chins to see who came when the door was opened. Beyond them were more stacks of 'soft-goods.'

On each side of that columned interior was a gallery. Broad flights of steps on either side led up to these, with strong metal balusters on which porters, carrying great loads on their shoulders, could lay a hand to aid their balance. When Tommy Bruce first saw the galleries they reminded him of pictures he had seen of oriental bazaars. In the gallery-recesses to left and right (right: Wincey and Flannelettes – left: Dress Goods) were more columns of cloth among which one could see the warehousemen at work, and hear them, too – hear the voices antiphonally intoning words and numbers as in some strange rite.

The whole place was roofed with glass. In centre was what at first sight seemed like an enormous vat of polished wood but, on advancing towards it, it revealed itself as what, in warehouse parlance, was 'the well.' Looking down there, one had a glimpse of the calender-man's bald head in a haze of fluff rising from some bolt of cloth quaking through his mangle-like machine. To left was a door leading into the receiving and despatching chamber where was a hoist that rose and fell by hydraulic power between that floor and the basement.

A flight of stairs, there, also gave access to the basement – the packers' quarters and old Fenwick's. At the far end of that chamber heavy broad doors opened into the cobbled court, where the lorry horses tossed their nose-bags and pigeons fluttered and pottered, pecking at the scattered dole, while loading or unloading was in progress.

In that rear court, into which the lorries backed with a great clash of iron-shod hoofs, when the bosses were out, employees 'dying for a smoke' would sometimes stand for five minutes having a whiff of tobacco – for the head-packer would permit no one to come to his basement for that. He was king down there, and in direct Doric, or in what Dunbar called 'our ancient Ingliss', if he smelt tobacco-smoke coming from the little room in the far corner, he would hammer on the door and tell whoever was inside what the place was for, and that it was 'nae' smoking-room.

from *The Staff at Simsons*, Frederick Niven, 1937

Ebenezer Moir was in a preoccupied condition in his Glassford Street ware-house. He sat in his private room. Its window was the middle one of three (near the corner of Wilson Street) that showed green glass half-way up, and ordinary glass beyond – the one on which the name *Moir* appeared in gold letters. The long window north had the word *Ebenezer* upon it; the other one south read *Manufacturer*, and below, in the corner, in small letters – *And in Bradford, Yorks*.

He rose. Caird returned to his desk, and Mr Moir swung into the ware-house, passing through its departments with heavy tread. He visited the Shirtings, Flannelettes, Winceys, nodding to his heads of departments. Some had matters of business to discuss with him, but seeing his manner they knew he was not in a talking mood. The head of the Flannelettes, who paid no heed to moods, a rough, honest, broad-talking man, pleasantly vulgar, tried to detain him.

'Oh, later on, later on,' said Mr Moir abruptly.

All right, sir.'

He ascended to 'The Looms,' as the great attic was called where, on hand-looms, new designs were woven to see how they looked before going farther. He stood listening to the clitter-clatter of the flying shuttles. Very seldom did he mount up there, and the weavers who saw him wondered what brought him so high. He stood behind one of the men watching the shuttle fly to and fro, as if fascinated by it – or perhaps on the verge of saying: 'Oh, stop that design! It's no good!' There was a suggestion of rage on his face.

from *Justice of the Peace*, Frederick Niven, 1914

Glasgow became for a time last century quite a 'clubby' place for the business fraternity, and most of these establishments were close to Buchanan Street.

The Western Club stands at the corner of St Vincent Street and Buchanan Street (opposite, by the way to the unofficial Press Club in Cairns' public-house). It is a very smart club, perhaps the only one in Glasgow which is in any way exclusive.

The Art Club, a place by rights of sweetness and light, is in Bath Street, which, as the home of doctors, is known, appropriately enough, as the Valley of the Shadow of Death.

The Liberal Club, again, adjoins a hotel in an unfashionable part of Buchanan Street, but, on the other hand is opposite the Subway Station and near the Athenaeum, a place of cheap culture.

The Conservative Club is in Bothwell Street, and its very, very large building may have caught its look of a store for sanitary appliances from being situated opposite to a shop occupied by Messrs Doulton & Co. Ltd. (of London, Paris and Paisley). It is famous for lunches, this club, and on the days when the Tharsis Copper Company declares its dividend, there is served, they say, in a private room and to shareholders only, a meal which would pervert a vegetarian. Otherwise the building is convenient for both Central Station and Hengler's Circus.

The New Club has a most imposing house in West George Street, in a wilderness of banks and offices. It has rather the air of being about to fall into the street, and for this reason, perhaps, you never see anyone at the front windows.

from *Glasgow in 1901*, J H Muir, 1901

'J H Muir' was in fact a pseudonymous name for three friends who collaborated to produce some of the best descriptive writing about Glasgow of their period. James Bone was a noted Fleet Street journalist; his brother Muirhead Bone (later Sir Muirhead) was a water-colourist and etcher; and Archibald Charteris, a lawyer.

They identified a rather more douce aspect of the Glasgow character than that which was on display on raucous Saturday nights:

It is not the accent of the people, nor the painted houses, nor yet the absence of Highland policemen that makes the Glasgow man in London feel that he is in a foreign town and far from home. It is a simpler matter. It is the lack of tea shops. . .

from *Glasgow in 1901*, by J H Muir, 1901

He descended to the rattle and buzz of the city, strolled down Buchanan Street, a quiet street underfoot at this end, easier on the ear-drums than it is at the top of the hill where the lorries rattle over stone in the region of St Rollox; timed his watch at Edwards' clock – with 'Greenwich Time' written above it. A faint, red, afternoon fog was coming over the city. It stained the white casement curtains in a tea-shop of Buchanan Street, and, as he noticed that delicate stain upon them, like an atmospheric dye, it struck him that he saw it wonderfully well.

As he paced westwards, he was pleasantly importuned by the odour of newly-ground coffee-beans. His heart stirred; and instead of going on to Gordon Street and the homeward train, he disappeared abruptly from the pavement; he had dived down to his sanctuary, the tea-house in Ingram Street.

Tonight there was nobody in the smoking-room when he descended. The felt-slippered waiter, in ordinary lounge suit, brought coffee and cigarettes, set the polished match-box and ash-tray, stood beside him chatting; then, having laid an illustrated weekly beside him, departed.

Not a sound was to be heard but that of footsteps in the street as homing people trod over the dulled bull's-eye lights set before the window in the pavement instead of gratings; just that – and anon the sound of coffee-grinding again, or it might be knife-cleaning, or of the working of the air-cleansing apparatus. At any rate it did not jar the quiet. A feeling of exaltation came to

The Herald

Craig's smokeroom and picture gallery in its Gordon Street basement on the day of its closure on 2nd April 1955

him. This might be what Walt Whitman meant by 'I loaf and invite my soul.' There was much of subdued richness, to Martin's eyes, in this deserted smoke-room. It was like reproductions of Velasquez – rich and sober and velvety. The door opened gently and two men entered, talking quietly, and took seats at a far table. The waiter drifted in to them, listened to their low-spoken order, drifted away. They spread a chess-board before them, set up the pawns, the kings, the queens and the knights all in order, and slowly Martin slipped the sketch-book out, and began to draw again.

from *Justice of the Peace*, Frederick Niven, 1914

Argyle Arcade (the principal, extending from Argyle Street, between Buchanan and Queen Streets, to Buchanan Street) consists of a double row of shops and saloons of two flats, covered in with a plain glass roof. It forms a much-frequented promenade, and is especially convenient for ladies shopping in the neighbourhood. If the day be showery they find a shelter, and still have the pleasure of inspecting the latest novelties in sundries, as the shops are all of a very good class. Among its saloons there is the Argyle Café and Dining Rooms, where a very fair dinner can be had at the ordinary rates; and Reid's, at the central corner, is a favourite luncheon-place with many of the ladies.

from *Kirkwood's Dictionary of Glasgow*, 1884

He preferred coffee every time. He enjoyed going up to town on Saturdays to buy a half-pound of the real stuff. The old polished oak shop in Renfield Street – with its overflowing sacks of beans and crystallised ginger in jars richly painted with Chinese dragons – had a grinding machine that produced

The Herald

The entrance to the old Argyll Arcade early in the century. The shops flanking the entrance are Hunter and Company on the left and Stuart Cranston's Tearoom on the right

the velvet smell of coffee as well as the smooth brown powder. A hundred delicate aromas floated in the shop, and together formed a warm drug cloud to anaesthetise and titillate the senses.

He lingered there, savouring the sight, the sound, the smell of the place for as long as possible, happy to pace around waiting while other people were being served, then happier still to burst into eager conversation with the old man of the shop. The old man always seemed genuinely pleased to see him and they spoke about new blends and methods of percolating, and little tricks like adding a pinch of salt or mustard; it was as if no one had been in the slightest interested in coffee all week until he had come in.

The old man gave him pamphlets to study and Jimmy in turn searched out books from the libraries and the book-barrows on the history of the coffee-bean and the use of coffee, and the coffee-drinking habits of people all over the world, and he loaned them to the old man.

from *The Breadmakers*. Margaret Thomson Davis, 1972

IT IS QUITE A MISTAKE

To suppose that **STUART ORANSTON** SELLS ONLY HIGH-PRICED TEA, ranging from 2s. 6d. up to 4s. 3d. per lb. Such Teas as he deals in not one Family Grocer or Wholesale Tea Dealer in a thousand has the courage to buy— but it is the simple truth that he sells the BEST VALUE that MONEY and THIRTY YEARS' EXPERIENCE can offer at

1s., 1s. 3d., 1s 6d., 1s. 9d., and 2s. per lb.

A careful comparison of these Teas with any Blend in the Kingdom at from 2d. to 4d. per lb. more money will be a revelation to the consumer, and prove that

STUART CRANSTON

has the Cream of the Market to select from, and that he sells at one half the profit exacted by the largest dealers, who make the loudest pretensions.

76 ARGYLE ST. (Corner of Queen St.),
AND
28 BUCHANAN ST. (Corner of Arcade),

The Mitchell Library

Advertisement for Stuart Cranston's tearoom, from 'Quiz'

At the turn of the century, when there were attempts to establish 'reformed' pubs which would not adopt the 'hard-selling' of alcohol, there was a serious effort by the licensing trade to condemn the alternatives of tea and coffee:

> Coffee drunkenness is the last discovery of our medical friends. Working-class women of the great industrial centre of Essen are said to suffer from it very considerably. According to the British Medical Journal the cure includes 'small doses of brandy.' Promoters of the 'public house of the future' will do well to make a note of this. As they propose to abolish brandy and encourage the consumption of coffee,the future victims of the latter stimulant have a bad look-out.

from *The Victualling Trades Review*, 12 March 1890

Not all the clubs and coffee-houses were the exclusive preserve of the gentry, and it is a sad fact that the days of, for example, the public snooker hall have gone:

> Tommy Bruce raced along Cochrane Street to the square, down to Ingram Street, coasting the Union Bank, hurried down Virginia Street. Odours of foreign commerce were there being wafted from draughty entries and exhaling through pavement gratings, as was fitting to a street with such a name – odours of Virginia and the Indies. He turned the corner into Argyle Street, found the Argyle Rooms first and marched smartly into them. No, nobody there from Simson's; but to his amazement there were many young men sending the ivory balls kissing, cannoning, pocketing, some of whom he knew by sight – two from Knox's in Ingram Street, two from Ebenezer Moir's in Glassford Street.
>
> He hurried out and went on towards where, over the pavement, three enormous gilded globes gleamed. On the wall of the entry under these his eyes promptly caught the words *Cameron – Billiards*, and a somewhat crude representation of a hand with extended forefinger pointing upwards.

He mounted the stairs at a leaping stride. On the first landing, facing him, were swing-doors. The upper part of each was of frosted glass, and on each pane was the same word, so that the effect, at least to Tommy's mind, was of a joyous shout:

BILLIARDS   BILLIARDS

from *The Staff at Simsons*, Frederick Niven, 1937

Billiard tables are to be found in Glasgow in all the principal hotels, and in many saloons devoted to the purposes of the game; one of the best conducted of the latter, and where the best tables are to be found, is Green's, Renfield Street. Matches between professionals are often to be seen advertised in the daily papers, to attract notice to some new saloon. A visitor to a billiard saloon, unless a very good player, should under no circumstances engage in a game with a stranger however strenuously he asserts his inability to play.

from *Kirkwood's Dictionary of Glasgow*, 1884

Needless to say, there was a time when some public snooker halls were regarded as little more than illicit drinking dens:

Are you aware, my good sir, that there is scarcely a billiard saloon in Glasgow which is open after eleven o' clock that is not also a good-going shebeen. Within a radius of half a mile from where I write I can count up at least a score of billiard rooms where I can get a glass of execrable whisky at two or three o' clock in the morning. This sort of thing, too, goes on under the very noses of the police.

from *The Scottish Wine, Spirit and Beer Trades' Review*, 11 October 1887

'Poppies' was in a court behind Buchanan Street, along with a couple of abstruse businesses and an anonymous second-hand bookshop. It was the most recent example in Glasgow of a pub with adjoining disco, recent enough for Harkness not to know it. He knew 'The Griffin' and 'Joanna's' in Bath Street, 'Waves' and 'Spankies' at Customs House Quay. The pub here, 'The Maverick', was closed just now but the door to 'Poppies' was open.

As they climbed the stone stairs to the landing, they heard a droning noise. The double doors closed behind them in green baize. The motif was gambling. There were cushioned dice along the walls for sitting on. Each wall light held a poker-hand in glass. The floor of the small stage for the go-go dancers was a mosaic of a roulette wheel. At the end of the room the bar-counter was an enormous up-ended domino, double six.

'Love would appear to be a lottery,' Laidlaw said.

The noise was coming from a Hoover. The woman who worked it had her back to them. Context gave her an unconscious poignancy. She was elderly and fat. Each bare leg was a complex of varicose veins from too many children. Just by being there she was commenting ironically on all this jumped-up sophistication.

from *Laidlaw*, William McIlvanney, 1977

Martin was alone in the street, feeling elated, and full of daring. Packed cars jangled past; trace-horses loped down Renfield Street, the trace-boys sitting side-saddle on their backs were hitched on to waiting cars at the foot of the hill to help the two horses in the long, slow pull; cabs rattled to the station, showing glimpses of people in evening dress; a couple of soldiers went by, click-click, clickety-click. What a life! In the gutter drunk men argued; policemen eyed them, and then approaching said: 'Come on! Come on! Move on!'

What a day it had been – what a full-packed day! What an exhilaration was in his heart as he swung into the station, and the orange-lit clock showed him that in one minute a train should go. He sprinted up the platform in a sprint that brother John would have admired.

from *Justice of the Peace*, Frederick Niven, 1914

Sprinting into the station in a state of high exhilaration has pretty well been superseded by stumbling out in a state of geographical or cultural confusion, it seems. There is no doubt a certain indefinable series of emotions which get to work when you arrive at Glasgow Central after a protracted absence.

It was Glasgow on a Friday night, the city of the stare. Getting off the train in Central Station, Mickey Ballater had a sense not only of having come north but of having gone back into his own past. Coming out on to the concourse, he paused briefly like an expert reminding himself of the fauna special to this area.

Yet there was nothing he couldn't have seen anywhere else. He was caught momentarily in the difficulty of isolating the sense of the place. Cities may all say essentially the same thing but the intonations are different. He was trying to re-attune himself to Glasgow's.

There were a few knots of people looking up at the series of windows where train departures were posted. They looked as if they were trying to threaten their own destination into appearing. On the benches across from him two women surrounded by plastic shopping-bags looked comfortably at home. Nearby a wino with a huge orange beard that suggested he was trying to grow his own bedclothes was in heated debate with a Guinness poster.

'They'll no serve ye, sir.' The speaker was a small man who had stopped to watch the wino. The small man was in his sixties but his face was as playful as a pup. 'I spent an hour last week tryin' tae get a drink there.' He glanced at Mickey before moving on. 'Hope springs eternal in the human chest.'

It was the moment when Mickey arrived in Glasgow, in a city that was about proximity not anonymity, a place that in spite of its wide vistas and areas of dereliction often seemed as spacious as a rush-hour bus. He understood again the expectancy that overtook him every time he arrived. You never knew where the next invasion of your privateness was coming from.

from *The Papers of Tony Veitch*, William McIlvanney, 1983

But other passers-by have felt glad to be part of some mysterious, inexplicable social entity. . .

When he reached Union Street again and saw the two solid streams of human beings still mechanically flowing, apparently quite unchanged, although now different bowler hats, different cheek-bones and eye-sockets were borne on the dim surface under the misty electric lights, he took the first tramcar that came as though it were an ark riding an advancing deluge about to engulf him. And as he sat on the top of the lighted tramcar he felt somewhat as if he were in an ark, felt almost grateful to the other passengers for allowing him to join them, for picking him from the jaws of danger and taking him into this company of decent fellows.

Yet he did not speak to the man sitting beside him, for all those up here in this lighted, enclosed, moving chamber were united by a strangely intimate consciousness of one another, and all at once the knowledge came to him: They have all gone through it. And he was filled with pity for them, a pity quite without patronage, for he himself was included objectively in it. Yes, they had all gone through it. A great weight rolled from his heart.

from *Poor Tom*, Edwin Muir 1932

THE HERT O THE CITY
'In Glasgow, that damned sprawling evil town'
G S Fraser

I'm juist passin through
late at nicht. I risk a walk doun
through the gloomy tiled tunnel o Central Station
to Argyle Street and the Hielantman's Umbrella
for auld time's sake.

I see them at aince. Three girls and a wee fella
wi' a bleedin heid. He's shakin wi laughter
and the bluid's splatterin on the shop windae.

I'm juist about awa back up the stairs when they're
aa round me. 'On your ain?' 'It's awfu cauld!'
'Ye shouldna be here by yersel!'

I canna help but notice the smell o drink and dirt.
His heid's a terrible sicht.

I look round but I *am* on my ain.
'Whaur are you from?' 'Preston?' 'You'll know Blackpool?'
Soon he'll hae my haill life story out o me.

'You maun be cauld' and
'Ye shouldna be here by yersel.'

I offer them some money to get in out o the cauld
but they lauch at the idea. They're no hungry
and there's plenty wine left.

They'll get fixed up themorrow.
It's warm enough unner the brig.

They'd walk me back safe to my platform
but the polis'll be in the station.

'Ye shouldna be here yersel!'

Duncan Glen, 1976

I surmise that, very soon, the only way to get into the Glasgow Central Station and Hotel will be by parachute, or by subterranean passages under Gordon Street, Union Street, and Hope Street. That enormous block of buildings which occupies the site of old Grahamston village will soon be out of bounds for all timid and elderly pedestrians. I never approach it now but with my heart at my mouth. It almost scares me stiff to have to quit the pavements.

There is in Paris an intersection of two busy streets so fatal to pedestrians that it is known as 'the crossing of the crushed ones.' Up till now, by God's providence and my own agility, I have managed to steer with safety through the new maelstrom traffic of Crush Corner, Hope Street, but since the opening of George V Bridge to tramways I've lost my nerve.

Coming out of the Corn Exchange once I was invited by a friend to cross the street with him and have lunch at the Malmaison Restaurant. Hope Street was in spate with Mr Mackinnon's lovely trams and motor cars in a hurry positively homicidal.

from *The Brave Days*, Neil Munro 1931

So the horrors of Hope Street *do* go back a few years. Years which have allowed the over-indulgent 'rubber drunk' sufficient practice to survive an expedition into the city-centre arms of his preferred manifestation of Morpheus:

Across the street the door of the Corn Exchange opened suddenly and a small man popped out onto the pavement, as if the pub had rifted. He foundered in a way that suggested fresh air wasn't his element and at once Harkness saw that he was beyond what his father called the pint of no return. His impetus carried him into the middle of the road, where a solitary car braked and honked. He waved with an air of preoccupied royalty and proceeded to negotiate the rest of the roadway with total concentration and in a zig-zag pattern of immense complication. The road, it seemed, was a river and he was the only one who knew the stepping-stones. The car drove on slowly, the three women in it looking out to watch the small man threading himself through the station entrance.

from *Laidlaw*, William McIlvanney, 1977

AT CENTRAL STATION

At Central Station, in the middle of the day,
a woman is pissing on the pavement.
With her back to the wall and her legs spread
she bends forward, her hair over her face,
the drab skirt and coat not even hitched up.
Her water hits the stone with force
and streams across into the gutter.
She is not old, not young either,
not dirty, yet hardly clean,
not in rags, but going that way.
She stands at the city centre, skeleton at the feast.

Executives off the London train
start incredulously but jump the river
and meekly join their taxi queue.
The Glasgow crowd hurries past,
hardly looks, or hardly dares to look,
or looks hard, bold as brass, as
the poet looks, not bold as brass
but hard, swift, slowing his walk
a little, accursed recorder, his feelings
as confused as the November leaves.
She is a statue in a whirlpool,
beaten about by nothing he can give words to,
bleeding into the waves of talk
and traffic awful ichors of need.
Only two men frankly stop,
grin broadly, throw a gibe at her
as they cross the street to the betting-shop.
Without them the indignity,
the dignity, would be incomplete.

Edwin Morgan, 1978

GOVAN CROSS
IBROX
CESSNOCK
KINNING PARK
SHIELDS ROAD
WEST STREET
BRIDGE STREET
ST ENOCH
BUCHANAN STREET
COWCADDENS
KELVINBRIDGE
ST GEORGE'S CROSS
HILLHEAD
KELVIN HALL
PARTICK

For: Sauchiehall Street Centre; Glasgow Film Theatre; Theatre Royal; McLellan Galleries; The Tenement House; Glasgow School of Art; Royal Scottish Academy of Music & Drama; Stow College; Garnethill Synagogue

COWCADDENS WAS one of the earliest – and worst – slum districts in Glasgow. The name appears in various spellings in the 16th century as Kowcaldanis or Kowcaldennis: the area was regarded as swamp-land. The city's cattle-market and slaughter-house were established in the area, and were later replaced by a large nursery ground.

> Records of 1575 mention that Walter Gray had granted to him a piece of farm-land in the 'Common Bog' and this ground came to light during the construction of the Subway, with serious subsidences.
>
> from *Old Glasgow Club Transactions, 1900-1908*, James Steel

When the Subway station was constructed, at No 237 Cowcaddens Street, the area was still a slum. One account recalled that once there had been sweet pastures, '. . . which are now pied with anything but buttercups and daisies.'

> A constable led Mr Struan Ure Gordon off through the drab streets of the Cowcaddens to Mince Collop Close. This warren of ticketed houses was entered through a low archway, which was pervaded by the stench of ammonia. Against the peeling walls lounged seven young men of lowering, unfriendly aspect, who spat as they passed, apparently in tacit criticism of Constable MacLeod. They had to pick their way over a lively heap of filthy,

vociferous children at the dark entry to the narrow wooden stairway, which led them, the gnarled treads protesting, to a landing on which half a dozen frail doors opened. On one of these the policeman knocked. A panel of the door was stealthily removed; through the black orifice peered a swollen face. Then the door was opened by a blowsy old woman, in filthy bodice and short-gown, whose pale eyes widened as she fully recognised in the gloom the character of her visitors.

'Christ Almighty! The Cops!' she enunciated slowly.

from *Mince Collop Close*, George Blake, 1923

The address on the letter which Norah received from Sheila Carrol was '47 Ann Street, Cowcaddens,' but shortly after the letter had been written the Glasgow Corporation decided that 47 was unfit for human habitation, and those who lived there were turned out to the streets.

It was late on the evening of the day on which she left Jean and Donal that Norah came to No 47, to find the place in total darkness. She groped her way up a narrow alley to the foot of a stair and there suddenly stepped on a warm human body lying on the ground.

'What the devil! – Ah, ye're choking me, an old person that never done no one no harm,' croaked a wheezy voice, apparently a woman's, under Norah's feet. 'I only came in oot of the cauld, lookin' for a night's shelter. Hadn't a bawbee for the Rat-pit. Beg pardon! I'm sorry; I'll go away at once; I'll go now. For the love of heaven don't gie me up to the cops. I'm only an old body and I hadn't a bawbee of my own. I couldn't keep walkin' on all night. Beg pardon, I'm only an old body and I hadn't a kirk siller piece for the Rat-pit!'

'I'm sorry, but I didn't know that there was anyone here,' said Norah, peering through the darkness. 'I'm a stranger, good woman.'

'Ye're goin' to doss here too,' croaked the voice from the ground.

'I'm lookin' for a friend,' said Norah. 'Maybe ye'll know her – Sheila Carrol. She lives here.'

'Nobody lives here,' said the woman, shuffling to her feet. 'Nobody but the likes of me and ones like me. No human being is supposed to live here. I had at one time a room on the top of the landin', the cheapest room in Glasgow it was. Can't get another one like it now and must sleep out in the snow. Out under the scabby sky and the wind and the rain. It wasn't healthy for people to sleep here, so someone said, and we were put out. Think of that, and me havin' the cheapest room in the Cowcaddens.'

from *The Rat Pit*, Patrick McGill, 1914

Despite the grim nature of life in Cowcaddens in earlier times, the squalor was in close proximity to the grander parts of the city, and the 'Cowcaddens' address did not necessarily imply the worst:

The Theatre Royal in Cowcaddens took its place as the leading theatre. It had been erected in 1867 as a great music hall, called the Colosseum. It was opened in 1869 as the Theatre Royal, and was in 1879 entirely destroyed by fire, the loss amounting to between £35,000 and £40,000. The present Theatre Royal was then erected on its site, and was opened in the end of 1880. The auditorium, which contains accommodation for about 3200 persons, consists of three tiers of galleries and the pit. Behind the orchestra are rows of stalls, the door to which opens from Hope Street, and so is the upper circle. The pit and amphitheatre are entered from Cowcaddens. The outer vestibule is paved with tessellated marble, and the whole interior is handsomely and beautifully fitted up and decorated.

from *Groome's Ordnance Gazetteer, 1893-95*

The City Archives

A back-court at Dobbie's Loan in 1910, with a scavenger at work in the left foreground

Under the blazing gaselier, David had recognised more than one friend who might have offered him a lift. But he had avoided everybody. The play had thrown him into a strange, unaccountable excitement. He wanted to be left alone. For a moment he looked about him, wondering if he should go down into Sauchiehall Street and pick up a cab for himself. But almost at once he decided to walk. The theatre had been hot. The fresh air would do him good. He wanted to think. He turned into Cowcaddens and made his way towards New City Road.

He was now passing through one of the slums of the City. It was only Tuesday night, and he would have only himself to look to. Towards the end of the week, when wages came in, drinking and riot made this district impossible at so late an hour. Even tonight, as he hurried along, he passed one or two wretches staggering and roaring. Many dirty, barefoot children were still about. There was filth and squalor everywhere; and not a little misery. For in November of 1878 Glasgow was deep in trade depression. In this she was like the rest of the Kingdom. Businesses were failing everywhere. Banks were collapsing. The City Bank of Glasgow had been the first and greatest British bank to go. Its shareholders and depositors had been the victims of fraud as well as bad times.

Unemployment was mounting. There were rumours of war. Depression bred depression. And meanwhile the people suffered; just such hungry, haggard people as David was passing now.

from *Wax Fruit*, Guy McCrone, 1947

The 'flit' was always an important feature of life in Glasgow, as people strove to move to the tantalising 'better area'. But sometimes, the move, rather than up a ladder, was down a snake. . .

The removal almost shattered Annie's resolve. When the morning of the day that was to see them installed in the new house in Parliamentary Road dawned it seemed to catch her between two conflicting moods – one of curiosity and the other of regret. In the past she had not had cause to think that the flats of the Avenue were in any way superior to the flats of any other tenement in the city. Where one building was so like another it surely followed that one house must be like another. She tried hard to keep her mind centred on that theme. But when she visualised the new premises!. . . and her brain would persist in flashing the picture. . . she saw Parliamentary Road. A dismal main thoroughfare, peopled with women who wore shawls instead of coats and hats; men who wore mufflers round their necks, and who spat; dirty wee shops; a public house at every corner, and more between the corners. She saw the building in Parliamentary Road in which they were henceforth to live – dirty grey; the story of its window-curtains one of misery, or the carelessness of poverty, or both; a dingy stationer's, a remnant shop, an appalling second-hand furniture and rag store – these were the shops that supported the houses. Then the wide, clean Avenue flashed back again for comparison. She shut her eyes to dispel the visions. But the pictures were clearer in the darkness.

Had she been removing to another of the suburbs. . . Partick. . . or Springburn. . . or even back to the shadow of the Provanmill gasworks. . . she would have been enabled to anticipate the change quite cheerfully, might have welcomed it as a tonic and interest reviver, for she had been rather tired of the Avenue. . . of the close and its people. But to Parliamentary Road!. . . Townhead!. . . where, even in the days of bright Spring sunshine, a humid, dulling haze blanketed the district. The permanent miasma of slumdom!

from Tenement, John Cockburn, 1925

Edwin Muir wrote with great humanity and concern for the plight of the country in the 1930s. He had much to say about the slums of Glasgow, and the unique feature which resulted in a wide distribution of slums close to, and sometimes within, the more tasteful areas.

The slums not only penetrate the lives of all classes in Glasgow, affecting their ideas and their most personal emotions, perhaps going with them into their bedrooms, but also send out a dirty wash into the neatest and remotest suburbs and even the surrounding countryside, so that it is possible for one to feel that the whole soil for miles around is polluted. This is partly, no doubt, because the slums of Glasgow are distributed over a very large area and in a very irregular form, so that it is difficult even in the West End to get very far away from them. Some of them are on the outskirts, like Polmadie and Springburn; others occupy a large area of the centre of the town at either end of Argyle Street; the older part of the South Side is honeycombed with them from east to west; and there is another large area from the Cowcaddens to Garscube Road extending for a considerable distance into the north-west, which is the rich and fashionable quarter.

from Scottish Journey, Edwin Muir, 1935

One morning Thaw and McAlpin went into the Cowcaddens, a poor district behind the ridge where the art school stood. They sketched in an asphalt playpark till small persistent boys ('Whit are ye writing, mister? Are ye writing a photo of that building, mister? Will ye write *my* photo, mister?') drove them up a cobbled street to the canal. They crossed the shallow arch of a wooden bridge and climbed past some warehouses to the top of a threadbare green hill. They stood under an electric pylon and looked across the city centre. The wind which stirred the skirts of their coats was shifting mounds of grey cloud eastward along the valley.

Travelling patches of sunlight went from ridge to ridge, making a hump of tenements gleam against the dark towers of the city chambers, silhouetting the cupolas of the Royal Infirmary against the tomb-glittering spine of the necropolis. 'Glasgow is a magnificent city,' said McAlpin. 'Why do we hardly ever notice that?' 'Because nobody imagines living here,' said Thaw. McAlpin lit a cigarette and said, 'If you want to explain that I'll certainly listen.'

They walked into the Cowcaddens and entered a close where the narrow stairs were worn to such a slant that the foot trod them uneasily. Thaw grew breathless and leaned a moment on a windowsill. He could see the flat back of a dingy church across a window box in which the soot-freckled crests of three stunted cauliflowers rose above a clump of weeds.

On the top landing, Drummond pushed open a bright yellow door (the lock was broken), stuck his head inside and shouted, 'Ma!' After a moment he said, 'Come in, Duncan. I have to be careful in case my mother's at home. If she dislikes someone she's liable to retire to her bedroom and burn a pheasant's tail feather.'

'What does that do?'

'I shudder to think.'

Thaw entered the queerest house he had ever seen. Parts of it were very like a home but these lay like valleys between piled furniture and objects salvaged from scrap heaps, middens and junk shops. As he edged into the kitchen he felt threatened by empty picture frames, stringless instruments and old wireless sets. The ceilings were loftier than in his own home but there was no open space and no planning.

'Excuse the mess,' said Drummond. 'I haven't had time to tidy up. I'm hoping to get a studio nearer the art school soon.'

from *Lanark*, Alasdair Gray, 1981

As thousands of young men and women (many of whom are drawn from the country districts) are employed in warehouses and offices in Glasgow, lodgings have naturally become the homes of great numbers of them. The immense extension of the railway system of late years has thrown open a wide field to those in search of rooms; but as a central position is of importance to many, numerous lodging-house-keepers may be found within easy distance of places of interest in the city, or of business centres. A comfortable sitting-room, with bedroom, bath, and use of piano, can generally be secured in the suburbs or in the western part of the city, at prices ranging from 16s to £2 10s, extras included. The favourite order of lodgings with students and others of the same class, is a sitting-room with small bedroom, the latter often opening off the former. They usually are let at from 10s to 15s, and abound in the district intersected by the New City Road, and in Dumbarton Road. Baths are seldom to be had in these; and pianos, where there is one, are execrably out of tune, as a rule.

Before taking lodgings in any particular street, it would be well to consult some well-informed friend, or a respectable house-factor, as to its character.

from *Kirkwood's Dictionary of Glasgow*, 1884

Probably one of the most notable representatives of that confectionery industry of which the Scottish trade capital has become a first centre is to be found in the large and prosperous undertaking now controlled by Messrs John Buchanan & Brothers. As makers of confections, preserves, and peels, and producers of everything that can be now-a-days comprehended under that general category, Messrs Buchanan hold a place of unrivalled distinction.

Situated in so central and convenient part of the City as Cowcaddens, Messrs Buchanan's factory in Stewart Street may be said to be exceptionally favoured, and the range of the four-storey erections that compose the entire manufactory constitutes a great structural feature of this neighbourhood, in which the firm's industry has long formed an interesting and profitable source of work and trade.

The boiling room, which is probably the most important feature in a large confectionery, is well adapted for the operations carried on. It is fitted up with vacuum and other boiling pans, some of which have a capacity of three to four cwts, and is provided with slate and metal tables for the reception of the sweets when boiled. The pan room plays also an important part in the manufacture of sweets, and in it are seen a large number of revolving pans of every description. The same spacious and lofty features are noted in the lozenge room, the fondant and gum goods department, the stores for materials, the sugar mills, the peel making rooms, the preserve rooms, the jar washing rooms, and the rooms for the storage of fruit.

from an advertisement in *Strattens' Glasgow and its Environs*, 1891

I took her into the dark of a picturehouse and we kissed and cuddled in the back row of the stalls among several similar couples. This was not satisfying. My furtive squeezing and fumbling brought none of the quick passionate excitement I sometimes saw enacted on the screen before us, so when we came out at nine-thirty I said, 'Are you coming home with me?'

She said miserably, 'I'd like to, but I don't want to get into trouble.'

I said, 'I'm not a fool, Denny. I know what precautions to take.'

She said, 'It's not that. You see I live in a hostel where they lock the doors at ten. If I'm not back before then I get into trouble.'

I said grimly, 'So this is the end of our evening, is it?'

I stared at her accusingly until she whispered, 'Mibby I could say I missed the tram and spent the night with a girlfriend.'

I said, 'Fine!' and steered her firmly by the arm to Cowcaddens Underground, but when I got her into my room off Hyndland Road I was nearly paralysed by embarrassment and worry, because I had never before been all alone with a woman. I coped by behaving almost as if I was completely alone. I made a supper of toasted cheese and cocoa (for two instead of one), ate and drank mine, then brushed my teeth, and wound up the clock, and carefully undressed, folding each article of clothing into its proper place. She sat watching all this with an empty cocoa mug clutched on her lap. I did not put on my pyjamas. I took a contraceptive from a packet, showed it to her and climbed into bed saying, 'Come on, Denny, we arnae doing anything unusual.'

She said in a wobbly voice, 'Can I put the light out?'

I said, 'Please yourself.'

from 1982 Janine , Alasdair Gray, 1985

The Wellington and Queen's Arcades connect Sauchiehall Street and Renfrew Street with Cowcaddens. The shops are of the second-rate class, the arcades being principally used as a short-cut to Cambridge Street or Cowcaddens. They contain one or two old book-stalls, in which the connoisseur may find something worthy of notice.

The Royal Arcade connects the top of Hope Street with Cowcaddens Street. It is uncovered, and cannot be compared with any of the others, the shops being poor in appearance.

from Kirkwood's Dictionary of Glasgow, 1884

The City Archives

'The shops are of the second-rate class': The Queen's Arcade between Renfrew Street and Cowcaddens in 1960

115

As elsewhere in the city, when the 'poor in appearance' of the old Cowcaddens was swept away, the changes which were brought about did not immediately lead to better circumstances for everyone. The long and painful process gave rise to new miseries and exploitation:

'See a tenement due for demolition?
I can get ye rooms in it, two, okay?
Seven hundred and nothin legal to pay
for it's no legal, see? That's my proposition,
ye can take it or leave it but. The position
is simple, you want a hoose, I say
for eight hundred pound it's yours.' And they,
trailing five bairns, accepted his omission
of the foul crumbling stairwell, windows wired
not glazed, the damp from the canal, the cooker
without pipes, packs of rats that never tired –
any more than the vandals bored with snooker
who stripped the neighbouring houses, howled, and fired
their aerosols – of squeaking 'Filthy lucre!'

Down by the brickworks you get warm at least.
Surely soup-kitchens have gone out? It's not
the Thirties now. Hugh MacDiarmid forgot
in 'Glasgow 1960' that the feats
of reason and the flow of soul has ceased
to matter to the long unfinished plot
of heating frozen hands. We never got
an abstruse song that charmed the raging beast.
So you have nothing to lose but your chains,
dear Seventies. Dalmarnock, Maryhill,
Blackhill and Govan, better sticks and stanes
should break your banes, for poet's words are ill
to hurt ye. On the wrecker's ball the rains
of greeting cities drop and drink their fill.

from *Glasgow Sonnets*, Edwin Morgan, 1972

Of course, Cowcaddens has been significantly improved in recent years. The Royal Scottish Academy of Music and Drama is an important feature of the more pleasant face of the area and in early 1997 plans were announced for a multi-million pound Alexander Gibson Opera School as part of the Academy's future development.

GOVAN CROSS
IBROX
CESSNOCK
KINNING PARK
SHIELDS ROAD
WEST STREET
BRIDGE STREET
ST ENOCH
BUCHANAN STREET
COWCADDENS

ST GEORGE'S CROSS

KELVINBRIDGE
HILLHEAD
KELVIN HALL
PARTICK

*For: Scottish Ballet Theatre; Woodside Hall; Glasgow Youth Hostel;
North Woodside Baths*

THE ONCE-GRAND St George's Road leads from Charing Cross to meet Great Western Road at St George's Cross – or plain George's Cross to most folk. The Subway station was opened at No 39 Great Western Road. The Cross, on the edge of the Cowcaddens area, suffered – or benefited - from that proximity of tenement life and the factories and warehouses which supported it.

Ur ye sure we're oan the right line? In which direction ur we moving?

Dead straight, though bent. Like light. Curved, eventually circular. Darling round and round we go, round and round we go. . .

Always the same it is, nothin chynges. Fed-up wi' it ah um.

Too bad. There's no escape.

Nae optin-oot?

Opting out? Where to? To an unattainable Eden in our great cultured town? Paradise is lost, honey, lost. O serpent, serpent in damp basement, slither on to full enlightenment.

Sometimes ah wonder aboot you so ah dae.

Good. For without wonder we're lost.

It stinks down here.

And naebdy talks tae ye or even luks at ye.

Everybody an island. A wee Barlinnie.

Surrounded by litter.

O this our proud and native midden where everything's open and nothing's hidden.

Whit a come-doon – skyscraper tae underground, an headin' naewhere. Ye'd think thir wis a war oan or sumthin.

There's always a war on. Peace-time is a misnomer. We can't manage it for we're constantly at war with each other – and ourselves. Only great maturity and insight brings a kind of peace. And that has to be worked for real hard.

If thir's anither yin it'll be the last yin, that's for sure. A war.

Uneasy in peace, always preparing, we never learn.

Ah learnt early tae take it oan the chin and still grin.

Is that the reason?

Whit dae ye mean?

Is that the reason why the world's insane? O insanity, insanity, or do we mean humanity?

Ssshhh.

Ssshhh? Why should I?

Cause folk ur lukin at us.

Who cares? Let them. They might learn something that would help bring them out of their own narrow and inhibited little selves.

Like what?

Like thinking. Like taking an interest in the wider community. Like refusing to be exploited and manipulated. Like working on self-discipline. Like learning to eliminate that corrosive fear that steadily eats away at our distant and instinctive heritage of folk wisdom and roots. Like not being so spineless, passive and clueless. Like refusing to be divided. Like asking who, what, where, when, why.

Keep yir voice doon for god's sake.

Why should I when I'm only beginning to find it?

Cause people ur no used tae it. They luk up and keek and then luk away again. Deid embarrassed they ur. Deid embarrassed.

Except for that secret policeman taking notes in the corner seat.

Secret policeman? O come on. This is Glesca – European culchural city an a' that, no Moscow. We don't have secret polis in this toon. Run o' the mill cops, sure, but no secret wans. We're deid democratic an that.

That's comforting to know.

Is it? Good.

Glasgow. Great social security city. New Jerusalem of the north. Gleaming cultural jewel. Tiara for Tamara. Forget about debt and borrow for tomorrow. Have a ball in seasons of fine hel. . . Chekhov and piss-off. Blue socks in Ibrox. Bolshoi Ballet in the Dennistoun Palais. Pablo Casals doon in the Gorbals. O there's Berlin and Athens and Paris, and London and Venice and a', but if yese insist we'll tell ye whaur's best and it's no Bogota or Tokyo: for it's Glesca, it's Glesca, it's Glesca, dear auld Glesca toon, when yir oot oan

the batter in Glesca then ye don't mind the acid rain. . .
  Aw geezabrek wull ye? Whit's got intae ye ata', eh?
  The truth. The whole truth and nothing but the truth. I've seen the light.

Somewhere between St. George's Cross and Hillhead on the Underground, Jack Withers, 1988

Probably nowhere in this country has the equestrian business been better represented or brought to a condition of greater completeness and perfection than in the commercial capital. It is believed that perhaps the finest arranged stables in Scotland are those situated close to Charing Cross, Glasgow. The large premises of 120 and 122 St George's Road present a fine illustration of the standard of first-rate development to which a posting and hiring establishment can attain. The building is of three floors, and the interior, which is open in the centre, forms a square of 150 feet, the entire space being uninterrupted from the ground floor upwards. Stabling for the horses is afforded on two floors, while the ground floor affords ample accommodation for harness rooms, cab and carriage rooms.

The requirements of the stud are well cared for by a staff of efficient grooms, and the work progresses on all the principles characteristic of a first-class and well-equipped ménage. Between the branch establishment at Eglinton Street and the headquarters of the business communication by telephone is duly maintained, and the firm are at all times in readiness to carry out the most elaborate or urgent orders of a large hiring and posting business. Promptitude, which is at all times the essential element in funeral

The People's Palace

A fine photograph, c.1900, of St. George's Cross

undertaking, is observed in a manner thoroughly satisfactory to patrons, and the services of a fine stud of Belgian horses add to the impressive appearance of any large funeral *cortége*.

from an advertisement for James Robertson, Funeral Undertaker,Cab and Carriage Hirer, Job and Post
Master, in *Strattens' Glasgow and its Environs*, 1891

One of the greatest social scandals in Glasgow was the case of the infamous Madeleine Smith, who was accused of poisoning her French lover Pierre Emile L'Angelier in 1857. Smith was a daughter of a wealthy society architect; her 'unacceptable' lover was a poor warehouseman, who died in agony in his lodgings near St George's Cross. The case, which encompassed all the class distinctions of Victorian society, was notorious for the fact that it revealed that the wilful Madeleine had written letters to L'Angelier which, for the period, were regarded as highly scandalous.

[William Stevenson examined by the Solicitor-General]:

He had been four and a half years with Huggins & Co. I got notice of his death on the Monday forenoon from Corbet, a partner of the firm. I went to our place of business, then to the French Consul's office, where I saw Thuau, a fellow lodger of L'Angelier's. Thuau told me that Dr Thomson was L'Angelier's medical man. We went there, and got Dr Thomson to go with us to Mrs Jenkins's. We saw the body there. I heard of another medical man, a Dr Steven, having attended him; we sent for him, and he came. There was then no suspicion. The doctors said an examination of the body was the only way in which more could be known. I authorised that to be done next day (Tuesday). In consequence of the examination I informed the Fiscal. I did not expect L'Angelier to be in Glasgow on the Sunday night; that was inconsistent with his letter to me. When I went to his lodgings on the Monday I saw his clothes lying on his bedroom sofa. I examined them, and found on them various articles – a bit of tobacco, three finger-rings, 5s 7½d, a bunch of keys, and in his vest pocket were a letter and its envelope. I identify these. The letter reads –

Why, my beloved, did you not come to me? Oh, beloved, are you ill? Come to me, sweet one. I waited and waited for you, but you came not. I shall wait again tomorrow night, same hour and arrangement. Do come, sweet love, my own dear love of a sweetheart. Come, beloved, and clasp me to your heart. Come and we shall be happy. A kiss, fond love. Adieu, with tender embraces. Ever believe me to be your own ever dear fond,

Mini.

The letter was addressed Mr E L'Angelier, Mrs Jenkins, 11 Franklin Place, Great Western Road, Glasgow.

from *The Trial of Madeleine Smith*, edited by F Tennyson Jesse, 1927

Two local doctors were authorised to conduct a preliminary post-mortem at L'Angelier's lodgings in Franklin Place:

At the request of Messrs W B Huggins & Co, of this city, we, the under-signed, made a post mortem examination of the body of the late M L'Angelier, at the house of Mrs Jenkins, 11 Great Western Road, on the 24 March current, at noon, when the appearances were as follows:-

The body, dressed in grave clothes and coffined, viewed externally, presented nothing remarkable, except a tawny hue of the surface. The incision made on opening the belly and chest revealed a considerable deposit of sub-cutaneous fat. The heart appeared large for the individual, but not so large as, in our opinion, to amount to disease. Its surface presented, externally, some opaque patches, such as are frequently seen on this organ without giving rise to any symptoms. Its right cavities were filled with dark fluid blood. The lungs, the liver, and the spleen appeared quite healthy. The gall bladder was moderately full of bile, and contained no calculi. The stomach and intestines, externally, presented nothing abnormal. The stomach, being tied at both extremities, was removed from the body. Its contents, consisting of about half a pint of dark fluid resembling coffee, were poured into a clean bottle, and the organ itself was laid open along its great curvature. The mucous membrane, except for a slight extent at the lesser curvature, was then seen to be deeply injected with blood, presenting an appearance of dark red mottling, and its substance was remarked to be soft, being easily torn by scratching with the finger-nail. The other organs of the abdomen were not examined. The appearance of the mucous membrane, taken in connection with the history as related to us by witnesses, being such as, in our opinion, justified a suspicion of death having resulted from poison, we considered it proper to preserve the stomach and its contents in a sealed bottle for further investigation by chemical analysis, should such be determined on.

Part of the evidence of the first post-mortem, by Dr Hugh Thomson, from *The Trial of Madeleine Smith*, edited by F Tennyson Jesse, 1927

A second post-mortem was later held in the crypt of the Ramshorn Church, where L'Angelier is buried. Stomach contents were further examined by Professor Frederick Penny of the Andersonian University. He declared that L'Angelier had been poisoned by a massive amount of arsenic.

The trial was the subject of intense national excitement. Madeleine was eventually released after an inevitably controversial 'Not Proven' verdict. She became a member of the Bloomsbury Set in London and later emigrated to New York, where she died at the age of 93, apparently protesting her innocence – despite continuing rumours that she had admitted the poisoning.

One contemporary poem records the popular view of the scandal:

HEAVEN KNOWS

Lines on the Trial of Madeleine Smith for the Murder of L'Angelier

Shade of the hapless stranger, lost L'Angelier,
  Whose life's young light was quenched in guilt and shame,
Say, haunt'st thou still the lane, the fatal gate,
  Where to thy arms the fair, false syren came?

We seek not now thy 'merits to disclose,
  Or draw thy frailties from their dread abode';
We would not sit in judgement on the man
  Whose soul hath stood before the bar of God.

'Not Proven' was thy thrice-repeated deed,
  Thou of the stony heart and dauntless eye:
Smile not; in Heaven's high court thou yet shalt hear
  The unerring proven verdict of the sky.

A lovely isle lies cradled in the deep,
  Its flowery glades embowered in fruitful trees,
A weeping mother wanders on the beach
  And pours her sorrows on the seaward breeze.

Ah! to her widowed heart her only son
  She last had clasped upon that island shore;
He came, he saw, he loved, he sinned, he died –
  We wait till Heaven and time shall tell us more.

Janet Hamilton, 1857

St George's Road formed one of those areas in which the grubby side of Glasgow came close to the West End – a kind of 'half-way-house' in which one set of characteristics could easily rub off on the other.

Mr Alfred liked the week-end. He could forget school and Miss Seymour then. On a Saturday afternoon he went strolling along Sauchiehall Street. He meant to go to Boots and buy shaving-soap and razor-blades. But he was on the wrong side of the road, and when he came out of a daydream he saw he couldn't get across. Where there should have been four lanes of one-way traffic racing from west to east, with a break at Hope Street or Renfield Street on the Cross signal, there was only a crowd of pedestrians from east and west who kept going on a collision course. He thought it rather strange so many people should be walking in the middle of a busy road. It took him a moment or two to make out that what he was seeing was two gangs, about fifty in each, armed with axes and hammers, throwing bottles and yelling as they advanced.

He was frightened by the noise and the flourish of weapons. When the rearguards flowed from the road on to the pavement, routing the neutrals there, he ran into a shopdoorway. He wasn't the only one. All the shopping housewives flocked for cover, and their hysterical screams made bedlam of a battlefield already bellowing and rebellowing. He saw a scampering matron trip herself in her hurry and fall on her face just as an empty bottle crashed beside her. He was terrified, but he thought he had to be at least a gentleman if not a hero. He dashed from his shelter and tried to help her to her feet. She was fat and heavy. He couldn't lift her. He felt the sag of big flabby breasts as he grasped her round the middle and he blushed. Some women, gabbling indignantly, gave him a hand and raised their fallen sister. She got off her knees slowly, white and shaking.

When he had her calmed a little and taken her to the doorway Mr Alfred turned to watch what was going on in the street. He was still frightened, but he was interested too. He couldn't believe that two gangs had the cheek to pick Sauchiehall Street on a Saturday afternoon as the venue for a challenge match, Sauchiehall Street above all places, the city's most famous thoroughfare, its answer to Edinburgh's Princes Street, to London's Regent Street.

from *Mr Alfred MA*, George Friel, 1972

The reputation of St George's Cross, never an entirely secure matter, took a further comic knock in 1971 when two armed men, having raided the Clydesdale Bank, decided to make their getaway by Subway. Of course, they were caught and were locked away from further underground excursions for ten years.

The Burleigh Hotel was at the West end of Sauchiehall Street. The architecture was Victorian and very dirty. It had been cunningly equipped with curlicues and excrescences, the chief effect of which was to make it an enormous gin for drifting soot and aerial muck. It stood now half-devoured by its catch, weighted with years of Glasgow, its upper reaches a memorial to the starlings that had once covered the middle of the city like an umbrella of demented harpies.

Braked by its draught-excluder, the big, glass-panelled door opened hesitantly, as if the place was coy about letting you in. The foyer was large, its sea-green carpet choking in a Sargasso of worn threads. It was hard for Harkness to imagine what might have done the wearing.

He trekked across the carpet to Reception. The keyboard held more metal than an arsenal. The pigeon-holes were crammed with emptiness. He couldn't see Laidlaw's name upside down on the register. He pressed the bell. It buzzed harshly, as if it was out of practice.

The woman who came out of the cubby-hole at the side was unexpected. A woman like her was always unexpected. She was mid-twenties, attractive, and she had that look of competence in being female that makes men count their hormones. She smiled once at Harkness and he wanted her to smile twice.

'I don't suppose you have a vacancy,' he said, nodding at the keyboard.

She had adjusted to the archness of his levity before he had finished speaking.

'This is our quiet year,' she said.

from *Laidlaw*, William McIlvanney, 1977

GOVAN CROSS
IBROX
CESSNOCK
KINNING PARK
SHIELDS ROAD
WEST STREET
BRIDGE STREET
ST ENOCH
BUCHANAN STREET
COWCADDENS
ST GEORGE'S CROSS

KELVINBRIDGE

HILLHEAD
KELVIN HALL
PARTICK

For: Kelvin Walkway; Park Campus, Glasgow Caledonian University: Glasgow University; Goethe Institute; St Mary's Episcopal Cathedral

KELVINBRIDGE is that area where Great Western Road crosses the River Kelvin. Before the present bridge was built in 1891, there were two bridges, one above the other.

Glasgow Rangers, formed in 1872, had their first football ground at Kelvinbridge, near St Mary's Episcopal Cathedral, before making their move to Ibrox in 1887.

The Central Hotel in town opened an annexe at Kelvinbridge in 1895. The superb red sandstone Caledonian Mansions was situated immediately at the northern end of the bridge, directly above the Caledonian Railway's Kelvinbridge Station, which was on a spur line into the centre of the city. If the Central Hotel was busy, visitors from the south would change trains at Glasgow Central and make for Kelvinbridge and the annexe.

When the Subway opened, Kelvinbridge was the only station to have two separate entrances, one at 433 Great Western Road, and the other under the bridge at 76 South Woodside Road.

Kelvinbridge was where the West End began and the grimness of the city centre was left behind: it was definitely one of the favoured areas to which to move.

The Glasgow Academy was instituted in the year 1846 for the purpose of providing for boys in the West End of Glasgow a full and carefully adjusted course of instruction such as is usually given in the higher class schools of both Scotland and England.

For the first thirty-two years of its existence this purpose was most satisfactorily accomplished in premises situated in Elmbank Street, but as years rolled by the Academy's reputation and popularity increased, and it became necessary to find larger and more suitable accommodation. An admirable site about a mile farther west adjoining the Kelvin and the Great Western Road offering itself, it was purchased and the present most hand-some, stately, and palatial-looking building placed upon one portion of it, the other portion being laid out and fitted as a play and recreation ground.

from an advertisement in *Strattens' Glasgow and its Environs*, 1891

For much of last century and part of this, that part of Great Western Road from Kelvinbridge to the Botanic Gardens and Kirklee was the venue for Sunday promenades, when the well-to-do would parade in their finery, passing the time of day with neighbours and other passers-by.

She looked at him and saw the adoration in his eyes. The restrained warmth, the reserve of motherhood within her reached out to this boy, her man.

'Danny! Danny!' she cried with a strange, pathetic little catch in her voice.

Into his arms she sank and rested there gladly, while her proud mouth was crushed by his kisses. Wanderers of the night passed them closely by, from the distant streets came the hum of the city's traffic, and the whistle of shunting trains in the great goods yard at Kelvinbridge tore through the night air. But they saw nothing but each other's near, dear faces, heard nothing but the beat of each other's hearts, till at last she withdrew herself from his arms and with a word, strangely curt, hurried away by herself on her last, mysterious mission.

from *Mince Collop Close*, George Blake, 1923

The Kelvingrove or West End Park lies along the banks of the Kelvin, between Woodside and Sandyford. Originally the park was only on the E side, and was formed from lands on the old estates of Kelvingrove and Woodside, purchased by the town council in 1853 for this purpose at a cost of £99,569. A portion of the ground was, however, set aside for feus in so judicious a manner that it affords fair promise of ultimately reimbursing the total cost. The lands comprise a tabular hill on the E side, with rapid slopes on the N and S, and a longer but still sharp slope on the W down to the Kelvin, from which there is an undulating rise to Gilmorehill with the University buildings. The portion of the ground on the W side of the Kelvin was acquired from the University authorities. The part set aside for feuing includes all the top of the hill to the E, which is now occupied by the magnificent houses that form Park Circus, Park Street, Park Terrace, and

Park Quadrant. The ground was laid out, and the walks, drives, and shrubberies arranged according to designs by Sir Joseph Paxton. On the crest of the high ground opposite Park Street West is a lofty flagstaff, with – at its base – a mortar and two cannons captured at Sebastopol.

from *Groome's Ordnance Gazetteer*, 1893-95

Still unlinked, they descended to the Kelvin by a long winding flight of timber-edged steps cut in the steep earth of the ravine. Quickly the sunshine was left behind, and they dropped into the damp, shrubby gloom. Then mounting the slight wooden bridge, so arched that it had slats nailed across for foothold, they stood in the sunlight once more and looked down at the

The Mitchell Library

Bridges, Great Western Road *from a watercolour by William Simpson RI*

stream. Among the willows leaning top-heavily over the swollen current, some of the longest twigs were already threaded with silver.

The water kept catching at their drooping ends and letting them go again. Two greyish swans stayed themselves on the swirling surface. The rank grass was sprinkled with a few scraggy hyacinths. Joanna wished it was more beautiful.

from *Open the Door*, Catherine Carswell, 1920

Kelvinbridge is one of the boundaries of 'the University area', the others being Byres Road, Dumbarton Road and Woodlands Road. Many and various are the facilities which have grown up to service the large student population. Although the area is becoming more 'gentrified', many of the student haunts have stayed the course.

from **BEFORE DARK** (for Douglas Dunn)

They are so confident, the young, who strut
 Through the avenues that once were ours;
 So sure of themselves, knowing the future is theirs;
So cool and relaxed, as they scale the sweet
 Octaves of love; so self-possessed,
 Desire not yet on the wane, or become lust.

A bell sounds. The end of lectures for today.
 They fan out across the pastures
 Of the city, filling the nearest bars
Or returning to bed-sitters, wearily.
 The old smells linger; in Gibson Street,
 Curry powder; stale urine, from the Pewter Pot.

In my mind it will always be early winter
 In this Victorian sector of the city,
 Its terraces squandered by the University,
Heaped with swept leaves, a rotting umber;
 Kelvingrove a vast litter-bin; children
 Playing, generation upon generation.

from *In the Kibble Palace*, Stewart Conn, 1987

Bel's day of pleasure was by no means ended. For after the meal, her husband, having looked out of the dining-room window, and having seen that it was going to be a fine afternoon, told his wife to get on her things, because – since he would not have much business to do this afternoon – they might as well take the green car out Hillhead and Kelvinside way and have a look round.

And so the part of the town that was to know them for so many years to come took note, perhaps for the first time, of a lean, distinguished man, clean-shaven but for his greying side-whiskers, discreetly dressed, with his black frock-coat, his grey waistcoat, his black bow tie and his shining tall hat. And on his arm a handsome woman in her early thirties, with a good, maturing figure in a well-fitting bodice and flowing skirt. A smart hat with a piece of white veiling falling elegantly behind set on a fine, fair head. A mouth whose continual smile betrayed dazzling white teeth, and fine eyes that looked steadily about her.

Kelvingrove Art Gallery

'. . . solemn, liveried flunkies, sitting high above the spanking horses as they flew past brave, new terraces. . .' A description well-matched by Muirhead Bone's pencil drawing of Great Western Road in 1910

They had come, these two, to find their new home, and they found it in Grosvenor Terrace. A Victorian row, 'commanding a beautiful view of the brilliant parterres of the Botanic Gardens, with the umbrageous woods of Kelvinside beyond,' set back from the placid, easy-going traffic of a Great Western Road, where once in a while a green car rattled past on its way to and from Kirklee; where handsome equipages with their freights of silks and parasols glittered by on fine afternoons; the solemn, liveried flunkies, sitting high above the spanking horses as they flew past brave, new terraces, built of the famous Giffnock stone – cream coloured, and not yet blackened by the smoke of the encroaching city; where milk-carts jingled in the early morning, as they came from the country or passed back in the forenoons out to the green farmlands that lay so near at hand. A Great Western Road, where there was a good deal of mud in winter; and where – in the autumn – fallen leaves lay thick.

from *Wax Fruit*, Guy McCrone, 1947

BY KELVIN WATER (for Iain Crichton Smith)

I stood on the bridge
above Kelvin water
(the banks are prohibited)
and saw a piece of muddy ground
for cars to park,
an old man
who hadn't made it
to the subterranean toilet,
dribbling and cursing
in perpetual, mumbled rage,
the children playing
round the backs,
where the rats are,
and on the horizon,
where I expected the prehistoric cranes
of the dead shipyards,
I saw no horizon
but smoke,
and smoke so thick
and permanent
it will outlast the people.

There were trees
and a blackbird, female,
with a white head,
not singing;

from the under-arch of the bridge,
the flash of a wagtail.

In the vaults of the City Chambers
they were perhaps giving approval
to a new skyscraper housing estate
without any people,
or banning another film,
eating a dinner,
working on a plan
for prisoners
to pay rates.

'This life that we love and share.'

Below me the river heaved along,
carrying the weight of six days rain,
dead leaves, old tyres, and contraceptives,
splashing up brown, discoloured phlegm
from its poisoned depths.

Tom McGrath, 1972

There seems to have been something of a fascination among Glasgow
writers for tram and bus conductors, no doubt due to the popularity of
the job in the past as a summer refuge for students. Kelvinbridge seems
as good a place as any to meet them.

THE CAR CONDUCTOR

Ach! I'd raither be a cairter wi'
    a horse an' coal briquettes,
Or an interferin' polis catchin'
    bookies makin' bets,
But tae staun a' day collectin'
    maiks an' gettin' tons o' lup
Frae auld wives an' cheeky wee-
    men – man, it fairly feeds me up!

Wur first run in the mornin' wi'
    a lot o' silly goats,
Doon tae Yoker an' Kilpatrick,
    whaur they mak' the iron boats;
They smoke an' spit an' argy wha
    is likely tae get in,
Exceptin' when they're narkin' ower
    the heid o' Jimmy Quin.

But they're angels, bloomin' angels, compared wi'
    whit I get
In the efternune an' evenin – mair pertikler if it's
    wet;
Auld wives oot daein' shoppin', an' as nesty as can be,
When they're cairret on tae Partick an' them wantin'
    Polmadie.

Ach! I'd raither be a cairter wi' a horse an' coal
    briquettes,
Or an interferin' polis catchin' bookies makin' bets,
For I'm seik o' cheeky weemen, wi' their impidence
    an' fuss,
An' the Corporation, they can – richt, Wull. Here's
    the terminus.

from *Glasgow Types*, Charles J Kirk, 1910

I was twenty-one. I had just left university after completing a degree in English. I knew nothing. I wanted to be a writer. I was working on the Glasgow buses as a conductor, to see life. Later, I intended to work on the night-shift at a power-station like William Faulkner and write my first novel. That would take about six weeks.

But at the moment I was sitting on the back seat of a double-decker bus smoking a Sobranie Straight Cut cigarette. Opposite me sat my regular driver, Sardar. He was reading the Manchester Guardian. Not for the first time, I thought we were a strange pair to be in charge of a Glasgow bus.

I liked these day-time rests at the terminus. Passengers were few. The city had a peaceful semi-deserted look in the sunlight. The inhabitants seemed to consist of old people, young mothers and infants. Later it would be very different, as successive waves of truculent humanity invaded the bus at their appointed hours.

'Has he died yet, Sardar?' I asked.

The paper shook like a white flag in a breeze and then collapsed to show Sardar looking at me. He was never quite sure how to take my interest and always began by studying my face carefully for signs of mockery.

'He is my man,' he said. 'He fights for freedom.'

'Is he related to you, Sardar?' I knew that he wasn't, but the question would lead to further conversation.

'Sardar Singh. My name and his name. But we are not related. All Sikhs are called Singh. Did you know that?'

'Yes.'

He studied my face. 'Do you know what it means?'

'It means "lion".'

'Ah, but "Sardar"?'

'No.'

'It means "chief". I am "Chief Lion",' he said with emphasis.

from *Pride of Lions*, Geddes Thomson, 1985

Midway through the 2nd part of the shift an Inspector rapped the door. It was a different Inspector and they were at a different terminus. Reilly had left the cabin to go down the aisle checking for dropped coins beneath the seats. He muttered, O fuck, while returning to open the doors. Hello Inspector.

You're no due here for another 11 minutes driver I'll have to book you.

From the rear seat Hines cleared his throat. Glancing at him the Inspector turned to Reilly: Does your conductor always sit with feet on seats? When Reilly didnt answer he continued: 11 minutes, how did you manage it?

To be honest with you I never knew we were sharp till we got here. We only lifted half a dozen punters since Union Street.

The Inspector snorted. And he brought a pencil out from where it had been wedged behind his ear and beneath his hat; he flicked through the pages of his notebook then looked at Reilly.

Reilly, William, 6214.

Hines coughed. The Inspector stared at him. I told you before son get your bloody feet off that seat – people have got to sit there for your information.

Hines swivelled round; his boots clattered to the floor.

Come here.

Me you mean?

The Inspector continued to stare at him.

Hines rose, he walked up the aisle with his hands in his trouser pockets, and he stood closeby the Inspector.

Your waybill conductor, I want to see it.

It's in the waybill holder. Hines gestured towards the luggage-compartment. Then he got the waybill when the Inspector nodded at it.

Okay son, read me the numbers from your machine. Better still, let me see them for myself.

Reilly coughed as Hines raised the machine so that the Inspector could check the numbers there were corresponding to the last waybill entry. I'm not cheating the ratepayer if that's what you think.

I'm no saying you're doing anything. The Inspector sniffed and nodded before returning him the waybill. I dont see your hat.

Eh.

Where is it?

In fact I've not got it with me this evening; my child's fault; he spilled a turreen of chicken vindaloo all over it. The wife had to leave it to soak. Still no dry when I was coming to report this afternoon. Smell of curry every-where too; the neighbours were in complaining.

Name and number? The Inspector turned a page in his notebook.

Hines Robert 4729. Am I being booked?

Incomplete uniform. What was your name again?

Hines Robert.

from *The Busconductor Hines*, James Kelman, 1984

GOVAN CROSS
IBROX
CESSNOCK
KINNING PARK
SHIELDS ROAD
WEST STREET
BRIDGE STREET
ST ENOCH
BUCHANAN STREET
COWCADDENS
ST GEORGE'S CROSS
KELVINBRIDGE

HILLHEAD

KELVIN HALL
PARTICK

For: Hunterian Museum and Art Gallery; Botanic Gardens; Glasgow University

HILLHEAD is contained within a loop of the River Kelvin. Its western boundary follows Byres Road, which runs from Partick Cross to Great Western Road. It intersects this at Queen Margaret Drive, by Botanic Gardens.

Most of the original estates of Gilmorehill and Donaldshill have been built upon by Glasgow University and the Western Infirmary.

Byres Road was originally formed through what was called the 'Byres of Partick' or 'Bishop's Byres'. An attempt was made last century to rename the road Victoria Road, but apparently the public would not stand for it. Today, the area is the centre of the University precinct, with the headquarters of BBC Scotland and the Infirmary in the vicinity. The name Hillhead is nowadays often taken to include neighbouring Dowanhill, where many of the grander mansions still survive, even if some of them have been sub-divided, or turned into commercial premises.

When the Subway opened, it was planned to construct the station at Ashton Terrace, but it was eventually situated round the corner at 250 Byres Road.

It was the part of Glasgow which most often became the focus of the aspirations of those who strove to escape the poorer areas of the city.

Across the Kelvin lies the district of Hillhead, the whole of which is of quite recent structure. The streets are wide and airy, and most of them have good houses; while there are a number of terraces, with grass plots and trees in front. Constituted a police burgh in 1869 Hillhead was annexed to Glasgow in 1891. To the W and SW of it are the large and important districts of Dowanhill and Kelvinside, entirely occupied by self-contained houses, either in terraces or detached villas, these districts forming two of the most aristocratic quarters of suburban Glasgow.

from Groome's Ordnance Gazetteer, 1893-95

The cab jogged its way westward. Cathedral Street, Bath Street, Bath Crescent. The further end of Sauchiehall Street. David, though he was now twenty-seven and considered himself a man about town, was beginning to suffer from social panic. Each street, as he watched, sitting forward in his seat, seemed to have become incredibly short. The very outline of the new University seemed majestic and forbidding; seemed to belong to a world that was not his. Now he was outside the boundaries of the City of Glasgow.

The Hayburns occupied one of the many new-built mansions in Dowanhill. This pleasant preserve of the wealthy was coming into being. It took the cabman some time to find the house. For Dowanhill was then no less confusing than it is today. David, paralysed with shyness, hoped he would have to go on searching for ever. But at last the house was found. Now he must descend, preserving as best he might the outer semblance of a man of the world.

from Wax Fruit, Guy McCrone, 1947

Kelvinside Ladies College was established for the purpose of providing for the Young Ladies living in Kelvinside and adjoining districts as complete and high-class a course of English education as could possibly be secured, by the appropriation of the best and most salient features of a Continental curriculum, by a wisely arranged and carefully graduated course of study, and by enlisting the sympathy and talent of an eminent staff of teachers.

Kelvinside is generally acknowledged to be the most salubrious and fashionable of all Glasgow's suburbs, and here, occupying one of its finest and most elevated positions, surrounded by the most pleasant and beautiful of its natural associations, this College for Young Ladies stands as a centre of educational light and life and the prolific source of intellectual stimulus and activity.

The building itself, which overlooks the extensive pleasure grounds reserved for the use of the families residing in Athole Gardens, is a very commodious and comfortable one and seems splendidly adapted for the efficient carrying on of a large and first-class school.

The method of Instruction adopted by Mr and Mrs Widmer is, as far as practicable, that followed by the best German *Tochterschulen*; and, entrusted to the care of a numerous and thoroughly competent staff of teachers, it has been found to answer admirably. The curriculum, in addition to the ordinary

English subjects, includes thorough instruction in conversational French and German, science, needlework, class-singing, musical drill and health exercises; whilst, among the extra subjects, special attention is given to the various branches of music, drawing, painting, calisthenics, dancing, deportment, etc.

The neighbouring Botanic Gardens and the West End or Kelvingrove Park, both of which can be reached from the College in a few minutes, offer ample opportunities for healthful recreation and amusement.

Mrs Widmer is, we understand, at home every Tuesday for the purpose of receiving visitors on matters pertaining to the school, and would, we are sure, be happy to give information as to fees, etc.

from an advertisement in *Strattens' Glasgow and its Environs*, 1891

The Royal Botanic Gardens in Kelvinside, on the N side of Great Western Road, were long carried on by the Royal Botanic Institution; but, owing to lack of support, this society became involved in pecuniary difficulties, and the feuing of the ground was only avoided by the aid of the Corporation of the unextended city of Glasgow. When the extension of the municipal boundaries took place in 1891, the Gardens passed into the full possession of the city as one of the public parks, and they have since been extended by the incorporation within them of the open slope on the E side of the Kelvin. Part of the ground is laid out for the benefit of students with collections of plants arranged in natural families and orders, and there are also large ranges of conservatories. To the NE of the main entrance – close to which is one of the stations of the Central Railway – is the Kibble Crystal Palace, erected here in 1872 and extended in 1874, and taking its name from the donor, Mr. Kibble. There are two domes rising to a height of about 40 feet, while the larger is about 150 feet in diameter. Originally used as a concert and lecture hall, it is now appropriated for use as a winter garden. The present garden, first laid out in 1842, and enlarged in 1875, took the place of an older one formed in 1819 off Sauchiehall Road, now Sauchiehall Street, and that in its turn had replaced the original Botanic Garden at the old College.

from *Groome's Ordnance Gazetteer*, 1893-95

The Kibble Palace was used for many years as a venue for concerts and important public events; Disraeli and Gladstone both gave speeches there. The Botanic Gardens had a railway station, on the line which came out from Central Station, under Kelvingrove Park, to Kelvinbridge. Part of the original station buildings became the 'Silver Slipper'.

PERIOD PIECE

Hand in hand, the girls glide
Along Great Western Road.

                                Outside

The Silver Slipper the boys wait,
Trousers flared, jacket-pockets
Bulging with carry-outs.

The girls approach. A redhead pouts,
Sticks her tongue out,
Then passes under the strung lights
To the dance-floor. 'I'll have it
Off with that one.' 'Want to bet?'
'I'd rather lumber her mate. . .'

They nick their cigarettes.

                                Inside,

The miniskirts are on parade,
Listening to The Marmalade.

from A sense of order, Stewart Conn, 1972

Hillhead was one of the areas of the city to which generations of people had dreams of moving. Often, as the next extract indicates, the dreams were devolved on the children of those who experienced only a lifetime of disappointment in one of the more grim districts.

The genteel Hillhead-to-come was often a life-long obsession.

We lived in a mid-Victorian tenement of blackened sandstone in Warwick Street, near the Clyde, in the heart of the Gorbals, a bustling district of small workshops and factories, a great many pawnshops and pubs and little shops, grocers, bakers, fish-sellers and butchers and drysalters, tiny 'granny-shops' – where at almost any hour of the day or night you could buy two ounces of tea, a needle, *Peg's Paper* and *Answers*, a cake of pipeclay, a hank of mending wool – public baths and a wash-house, many churches and several synagogues. The streets were slippery with refuse and often with drunken vomit. It was a place of grime and poverty, or rather various levels of poverty and, in retrospect, an incongruous clinging to gentility, Dickensian social attitudes and prejudices.

In the late Nineties and the early years of the present century the Gorbals was a staging post for the westward surge of emigrants, mainly Jewish, from the Russian and Austrian Empires to the United States. For Jews the motive was escape from oppression, and economic only because of the hope that almost anything found in the west must be better. Poignant anecdotes from *der heim* – the ghetto of origin – constantly overheard, seared into the brain;

of casual pogroms with their cold, Dantesque brutality, routine rapes, floggings, merciless discrimination, extortion both financial and sexual.

Many of the exiles went no further. Those who prospered moved as far as they could from the Gorbals to what were considered more refined districts like Langside, Kelvingrove and Hillhead. For the rest the Gorbals was a social and economic sump which they could hope to escape only vicariously, through sons and daughters.

from *Growing up in the Gorbals*, Ralph Glasser, 1986

But maybe Hillhead was a little snobbish. . .?

You may suspect that Hillhead was an easy-going sort of place – and so it was, in a way. Yet in another way, it was, though not unhomely, a superior sort of place, the inhabitants generally being both bein and douce – two words with delicacies of meaning not to be gained from the dictionary.

The Mitchell Library

Employment in Hillhead *cartoon from 'Quiz', January 1896*

It would seem that they were not without a certain naive snobbery. Many of them did not wish to be identified with a common Street, and nearly every street was divided up into Terraces, Places, Buildings – you may yet discern the faded gold lettering on certain corners – and nearly everybody declared his or her address accordingly, to the confounding of stranger visitors.

. . .the first home of which I was conscious, was at 3 Great Kelvin Terrace. Why 'Great' I have never been able to comprehend; for it is a short row, and the houses are not mansions. We continued to use the grander address till, on a soaking Saturday night, at an hour that would shock us today, my father encountered a weary, weeping little boy, with a laden basket, seeking vainly for some bumptious Buildings or pompous Place. Thenceforth, plain '8 Bank Street' was added to the notepaper, and all tradesmen instructed accordingly.

from *I Remember*, J J Bell, 1932

The name of the street was on a plate on the tenement wall. It was the right name, but it was a street. I checked the piece of paper and the name was right, only it was not 'street' but 'Gardens'. I went round the corner and there was another plate and it had what I wanted. I was back in business.

The Gardens began with one block of tenements. After that there were hedges with neat bungalows tucked behind them. I searched for some clue about the numbering until I was frustrated, exhausted and ready to give up if there had been anywhere else to go. When I got the right house, I found in the middle of the gate the number trickily worked in iron.

It was a house like the others; if you were absent minded, or hungry enough, you might have rushed by mistake into either of its neighbours and sat down to someone else's dinner. No lights showed, but then it was late. Nothing but the inertia of all the little decisions since I had fished out the fold of paper in the taxi made me open the gate.

from *Brond*, Frederic Lindsay, 1983

It was a dismal road for a girl to follow in the dark of a wet winter evening. In that part of Hillhead the dull respectable houses lie back from the street behind a screen of sombre bushes, and afford only grudging hints of light and warmth within. The gas-lamps are widely spaced and pallid, making ghastly shadows with the branches of lifeless trees and the corners of irregular walls.

But Lorna instinctively chose the most tortuous and least frequented route eastward. Her heart had jumped to her mouth on the first exit from the house at the sight of a motionless figure on the other side of the road – the mysterious figure of a woman, her face obscured by a dark shawl. Instinct would have turned her back – and she could never go back. She fought to control herself. There was a lot of distress in town then; they were turning beggars from the door every half-hour. A woman could do no harm. . . Lorna hurried on.

The road into which she turned first, if empty, was wide. There were no trees, only a fenced strip of grass running down the centre of the street. She crossed to the walk by this desolate garden and found her feet hammering on concrete. Involuntarily she looked over her shoulder. Again her heart went pounding; the woman was following. Or was it just the trick of the shadow beneath that low-swinging branch? It was horrible; confusing as well. Her ears could catch nothing above the throb of her heart. Imagination! But she quickened her pace, making now decisively for the risky but comfortable traffic of Great Western Road. She could get a car and take the seat outside in front, and hide herself till the proper time in one of the waiting-rooms at the station.

from *Mince Collop Close*, George Blake, 1923

Byres Road has for long been the busy centre of the Hillhead area, the University's 'Rue Mouffetard'. Student life, as everywhere, runs well into the night, and the area is a constantly-changing mix of bars, boutiques, bistros and general vitality – with the exception of the Salon, which sadly appears to be a lost cause.

STREET SCENE

The faces outside the Curlers
Explode like fat cigars
In the frosty air.

Even the newspaper-seller
Rocks on his heels, half-seas over.

And I don't blame him.
    As the pictures
Come out, scores of lovers
Head for their parked cars.

Two ladies whisper
Goodnight to each other.
Neither feels secure
Till on her own stair
She snibs the basement door
And breathes freely, behind iron bars.

from *A sense of order*, Stewart Conn, 1972

Above the station entrance, which was graced for many years by an unusual cast-iron portico, two Glasgow University professors, Barr and Stroud, opened their first optical engineering workshop. They later moved round the corner to much bigger premises in Ashton Lane (now occupied by the Cul de Sac cafe-bar) before eventually opening the world-famous factory at Anniesland.

The Herald

*The 65-strong workforce of Barr & Stroud's workshop in Ashton Lane
c.1902 showing a naval rangefinder on its roof-top mount*

Along with the loss of the Salon, which provoked considerable
upset, the West End has also in recent years lost the Rubaiyat, with its
magnificent etched mirrors. Despite petitions, the cultural vandals won
both those rounds. There is still a Rubaiyat (if not the original) but the
Salon remains an abandoned gem.

'Did Tony know a man called Paddy Collins?'

Gus tested the hotness of the coffee.

'That sounds familiar. I think he's mentioned him.'

'He knew him well?'

'Tony didn't know anybody well.'

'What do you mean? He was a loner?'

'Not by choice. He tried to mix. But he was oil and everybody else was
water. He just sat on the surface. He thought he knew people. He probably
thought every casual chat was soul-talk. He was naive.'

'In what way?'

'Look. You could show Tony's development geographically. Without
going outside Byres Road. And that's pathetic. You know what he did? When
he came here? He was here before me. We've talked about it often. He spent a
year in the Salon in Vinicombe Street. Just down the road there. Seeing some
pictures three times. Whatever they were showing, that's what he saw. If it
was Tom and Jerry, he was there. He was hiding from the shock of real life.'

Then in his second year he did his Captain Scott. He started to go into The Rubaiyat. Then The Curlers. Then Tennents. Do you know what I mean?'

Laidlaw thought he knew. The three pubs are all in Byres Road. He supposed Gus Hawkins meant that Tony's progress had been towards some idea of a working-class pub.

'Then he went beyond Partick Cross. He was Vasco da Gama. The Kelvin. The Old Masonic Arms. Next stop, outer space.'

'That's where he seems to be now. There must have been some indication of him being under pressure.'

'Everybody doing finals is under pressure. You don't need the doctor's bag to work that out.'

'You think that's all it was?'

Gus seemed to be savouring his coffee.

'As far as I know.'

from The Papers of Tony Veitch, William McIlvanney, 1983

OBITUARY

We two in W2
walking,
and all the W2 ladies, their
hair coiffed and corrugated come
with well-done faces
from the hairdressers.
We together
laughing,
in our snobbery of lovers,
at their narrow vowels
and strange permed poodles.
Locked too long in love, our eyes
were unaccustomed to the commonplace.
            Seems silly now really.

We two in W2
walking
down Byres Road
passing unconcerned
a whole florist's
full of funerals,
the nightmare butcher's shop's
unnumbered horrors,
the hung fowls
and the cold fish
dead on the slab.

We saw ourselves duplicated
by the dozen in the chainstore
with no crisis of identity.
Headlines on newsagent's placards
caused us no alarm.
Sandwichman's prophecies of doom
just slid off our backs.

The television showroom's window
showed us cities burning
in black and white but we
had no flicker of interest.
An ambulance charged screaming past
but all we noticed was the funny old
Saturday street musician.
   Seems silly now really.

We two one Sunday
at the art galleries
looking only at each other.
We two one Sunday
in the museum –
wondering why the ownership of a famous man
should make a simple object a museum piece –
and I afraid
to tell you how
sometimes I did not wash your coffee cup for days
or touched the books you lent me
when I did not want to read.
Well, even at the time
   that seemed a bit silly really.

Christmas found me
with other fond and foolish girls
at the menswear counters
shopping for the ties that bind.
March found me
guilty of too much hope.
   Seems silly now really.

Liz Lochhead, 1971

GOVAN CROSS
IBROX
CESSNOCK
KINNING PARK
SHIELDS ROAD
WEST STREET
BRIDGE STREET
ST ENOCH
BUCHANAN STREET
COWCADDENS
ST GEORGE'S CROSS
KELVINBRIDGE
HILLHEAD

KELVIN HALL

PARTICK

For: Kelvin Hall Sports Complex; Kelvingrove Museum & Art Gallery; Transport Museum; Kelvingrove Park; Queen Mother's Hospital: Western Infirmary; Yorkhill Hospital

WHEN THE subway system was being planned, the intention was to name this station Dowanhill Street. However, it was changed to Partick Cross, as a concession to strangers using the system. The station is reached via a passageway from Dumbarton Road, its formal address being at No 5 Dalcross Pass, 166 Dumbarton Road.

Confusingly, Partick Cross station was often referred to as Partick East, to distinguish it from Merkland Street Station, which was unofficially known as Partick West. Visitors must have been well confused since there were in the vicinity of the Subway three stations of the Caledonian and North British Railways, at Partick, Partick West and Partick Central!

The name Partick (at one time Perdyec, or Pertmet) apparently derives from the Gaelic *aper dhu ec*, meaning the place at the confluence of the dark river.

Partick became an autonomous Burgh in 1852, confirming its fiercely independent nature and, like Govan, in modern times manages to retain a character decidedly of its own. Three short extracts may help to convey something of that character:

Almost opposite the entrance gate to Yorkhill Estate, at the gate of the Archbishop's Mill (later known as the Bunhouse Mill), is the Bun and Yill House, with the date 1695 above the door. From 1810 to 1830 every Saturday

145

afternoon in summer the members of the Partick Duck Club met here to eat duck and green peas.

In Partick, until the middle of the 19th century, the drummer was heard every morning at 5 o' clock and at 9 o' clock in the evening. All public intimations were advertised by the drummer, who passed from street to street, halting every 50 yards and beating his drum.

On the first Monday of November 1912, at midnight, the Burgh of Partick ceased to be. While the burgh organist played 'Lochaber No More', the Provost's chain of office was removed from his neck, and as his robe was laid aside, the Provost said, 'There they lie, the abandoned habits of the Provost of Partick, taken from him by Act of Parliament.'

from *Old Glasgow Club Transactions: Partick Landmarks 550-1912*, William Greenhorne, April 1930

It would be a fine thing if some brave soul resurrected the Partick Duck Club, for the loss of such apparently eccentric gatherings from the towns of Scotland has been an undoubted deprivation.

Besides the University, the other great social institution which survives in this part of the city is the Western Infirmary, which has mended many a Friday night head and progressed to become a respected centre of sophisticated medicine. There have been recent proposals to replace it with a £100 million teaching hospital on another site.

Independent altogether of its usefulness as a clinical school for the alumni of Glasgow University, the Western Infirmary, being reared at Donaldson's Hill, when completed, will confer a great boon on the inhabitants of the West End of the city, and of Partick, Govan, &c. These districts have risen within the last dozen years or so into considerable importance, and the want of an hospital in their midst has for a long time been much felt. The idea of erecting an institution of the kind in another part of the city than that in which the Royal Infirmary is situated was first mooted by the University authorities, and the project of the new hospital, in its earlier stages, was conducted mainly in connection with the scheme for the removal of the University. A site was secured in the neighbourhood of the new college buildings, and plans for the building were prepared by Mr John Burnett.

In general, the two upper floors only are appropriated to wards, but in the western wing, where the ground falls considerably, part of the third floor also contains wards. The dispensary for out-door patients is in this wing. Ample accommodation is provided for stores, linen, &c., for the apothecary department, for the consultation of the physicians and surgeons, for the rooms of the superintendent and matron, the physicians' and surgeons' assistants, the nurses and other servants, and for several convalescent airing-rooms.

from *The Glasgow News*, 22 January, 1874

The Partick district was for long an area where many of the Glasgow Gaels settled, and the lilt can still be heard on the streets. Many of those who came to the city from the Highlands became shipbuilders and marine engineers. They also maintained that other passion. . .

. . . there was nothing in the world for him but the Game. He hurried home, hurried through his washing, and changing and eating, and, as if all the claims of family and hearth were nothing now, was out on the streets again half an hour before two o' clock, a unit of one of the streams of men converging from all parts of the city and from all its outliers on the drab embankments round an oblong of turf in Ibrox.

The Mitchell Library

A drawing of the 'Bun and Yill House' in Partick, 1827

The surge of the stream was already apparent in the Dumbarton Road. Even though only a few wore favours of the Rangers blue, there was that of purpose in the air of hurrying groups of men which infallibly indicated their intention. It was almost as if they had put on uniform for the occasion, for most were attired as Danny was in decent dark suits under rainproofs or overcoats, with great flat caps of light tweed on their heads. Most of them smoked cigarettes that shivered in the corners of their mouths as they fiercely debated the prospects of the day. Hardly one of them but had his hands deep in his pockets.

The scattered procession, as it were of an order almost religious, poured itself through the main entrance to the Subway station at Partick Cross. The decrepit turnstiles clattered endlessly, and there was much rough, good-humoured jostling as the devotees bounded down the wooden stairs to struggle for advantageous positions on the crowded platform.

Glasgow's subway system is of high antiquarian interest and smells very strangely of age. Its endless cables, whirling innocently over pulleys, are at once absurd and fascinating, its signalling system a matter for the laughter of a later generation. But to Danny and the hundreds milling about him there was no strange spectacle here: only a means of approach to a shrine; and strongly they pushed and wrestled when at length a short train of toylike dimensions rattled out of the tunnel into the station.

It seemed full to suffocation already, but Danny, being alone and ruthless in his use of elbow and shoulder, contrived somehow to squeeze through a narrow doorway on to a crowded platform. Others pressed in behind him while official whistles skirled hopelessly without, and before the urgent crowd was forced back at last and the doors laboriously closed, he was packed tight among taller men of his kind, his arms pinned to his sides, his lungs so compressed that he gasped.

'For the love o' Mike. . .' he pleaded.

'Have ye no' heard there's a fitba' match the day, wee man?' asked a tall humorist beside him.

Everybody laughed at that. For them there was nothing odd or notably objectionable in their dangerous discomfort. It was, at the worst, a purgatorial episode on the passage to Elysium.

So they passed under the River to be emptied in their hundreds among the red sandstone tenements of the South Side. Under the high banks of the Park a score of streams met and mingled, the streams that had come by train or tram or motor car or on foot to see the Game of Games.

Danny ran for it as soon as his feet were on Earth's surface again, selecting in an experienced glance the turnstile with the shortest queue before it, ignoring quite the mournful column that waited without hope at the Unemployed Gate. His belly pushed the bar precisely as his shilling smacked on the iron counter. A moment later he was tearing as if for dear life up the long flight of cindered steps leading to the top of the embankment.

from *The Shipbuilders*, George Blake, 1935

Very distinctly in the forefront of Glasgow's flour milling trade must be ranked the old-established and eminent concern of Messrs John Ure & Sons, whose magnificent new Regent Mills, Dumbarton Road, have no compeer in Scotland, and are probably without a rival in the United Kingdom.

Messrs John Ure & Sons do a most extensive business as flour millers and as merchants, for they are the agents in Scotland of one of the largest Hungarian flour mills, their widespread and influential connection extending to all parts of the Kingdom.

The mercantile department of the business is conducted in a spacious suite of well-appointed offices and counting-house, and, in addition to a large and efficient staff of clerks and correspondents, a number of energetic representatives are employed. For fineness, purity, and general excellence, the firm's flour is unequalled – a condition due, doubtless, to the great care and sound judgement exercised in the selection of the wheat and the splendid mechanical appliances at the command of the firm.

Mr John Ure was long a member of the Glasgow Town Council, and in 1881 he was raised to the chief magisterial dignity his fellow-citizens could confer upon him, and for three years he performed the onerous functions of Lord Provost with singular dignity and ability.

from an advertisement in *Strattens' Glasgow and its Environs*, 1891

Glasgow has held three great Exhibitions of art and industry (1888, 1901 and 1911) on the Kelvingrove site, between the University and Dumbarton Road.

On Saturday, 10 November 1888, the 'Groveries' – silly name for an International Exhibition! – had closed after a six months' season, during which Glasgow had 'let itself go,' and in the loveliest summer weather enjoyed all the gaiety of a metropolis. That Saturday, 118,000 people passed for the last time through the turnstiles into Kelvingrove to take farewell of Paradise. There was a feeling that this dark sea-born city would never be quite the same again.

We paraded once more the garden city of bright white palaces, domes, and towers; lingered on its terraces, and listened to the bands; savoured finally the delights of its café restaurants, the noisy pleasures of its queer alfresco entertainments. A myriad fairy lamps outlined the banks of Kelvin and the slopes of Gilmorehill; rockets showered their jewels; the glow of the 'Groveries' on the sky was visible far out in the sleeping shires.

from *The Brave Days*, Neil Munro, 1931

T & R Annan & Sons L

An Annan photograph taken from the University tower in 1905 looking S-W to the River Kelvin and Partick. Scotstoun Mill and The Regent Mills (or Bunhouse Mill) are easily identified on opposite sides of the Kelvin. Just visible across the Clyde are Govan Parish Church and Fairfield's Yard

MacKelvie and Conner walked down Moore Street towards their homes. Moore Street was the link between the respectable quarters of South Partick and its slum area adjoining the river. It was a busy street, giving entrance to the subway and leading to the ferry. It was also well supplied with public houses. The red-leaders were conspicuous in their paint-soiled clothes at this late hour of the Saturday afternoon. Everybody was clad in Saturday best: Saturday being an even more important day to be dressed than Sunday. Some of the slum girls were more flashily dressed than the girls from better working-class homes. A number of them were recognisably prostitutes, making for Hope Street and Sauchiehall Street to find clients among the lecherous and hot-blooded section of the middle class.

The subway entrance breathed out its stale decayed air. Immediately beyond, where they turned into Walker Street, a warm, odoriferous waft of slumdom met them. It was not a smell that could be escaped. There were identifiable odours of cats' urine: decayed rubbish: infectious diseases: unwashed underclothing, intermingled with smells suggesting dry rot: insanitary lavatories, overtaxed sewage pipes and the excrement of a billion bed-bugs.

from *Major Operation*, James Barke, 1936

SCHOOL FRIEND

A platform lad in a miracle world
of gritty railway steam
at Hyndland, Crow Road, Partick West,
he kept a penny Woolworth book
and captured all the engine name and numbers
the beasts that panted every night
within their glass and iron cages
awaiting his command.

Saturday lunchtime 'Any cigarette cards mister?'
to tram-borne clerks all homeward bound
for hot pies football cinemas
late night wireless by the fire
before the Sabbath sermon, the Botanic Garden stroll
cold ham and visitors to tea
when 'Railway Engines of the World' was the series
at fifty cards the set.

Like a Daniel he had bathed
in furnace heat through the frosty air
footplate free in the city night
turntabled to death and glory
steel connecting rods his lances for the foe
and the great wheels four-four-o
his chariot against the weakness of the world.

Once in the dark of a dying suburb
he roamed the ruined Blackpool train
flat beer stale cake forgotten fags
and dodged the railway police who searched
like goblins in the foggy dark.

Once he sent the fussy nine-ten chattering
gallus locomotive of the gas-lamps
to some romantic rendezvous
of spies and sailors
in a far moon-haunted Clyde-coast town.

Then he was flicked from the sky
below a bombers' moon
and his time was stopped
above a foreign town
and the world quietly moved away
on its deterministic rails.

Fumbles now and then the dog-eared fading cards
from the tin box by his bed
as if they were a rosary;
tells them over and over
with the white tight gloves he wears
to meet his love
who never comes.

Bill McCorkindale, 1975

Following the success of the Great Exhibition of 1888, The Association for the Promotion of Art and Music lobbied for a great new gallery. The Exhibition profits, together with public subscription and Glasgow Corporation funding paid for the superb new Kelvingrove Art Gallery and Museum, which was opened during the 1901 Exhibition.

Young Jason had so far spent over ten minutes staring in at the diorama in Kelvingrove Art Gallery and Museum, long enough for most modern kids who, weaned on television, tend only to snack on reality. But this quaint box of tricks, a cousin of the magic lantern and the flannelgraph, had the boy hooked. So there I stood, a prisoner of low wattage sunrises, watching the seasons come and go, seeing the stoat, the mountain hare, and the ptarmigan changing alternately from their summer garb to their winter one, then back again. It made me uneasy this gawping at the torrent of days as they disappeared down Time's plughole. This silent doombox, this cube of light, was a die rolled from a craps game in Hell. It served as a reminder that Time, Auld Nick's hitman, was up'n hustling.

Since we were in the galleries I decided, in a roundabout way, to satisfy the boy's notion to see a man-in-armour by taking him upstairs to view Rembrandt's masterpiece on that very subject. On our way there I'd explain to Jason that it was unlikely we'd come across any ice-cream vendors in the galleries, no, not even in the Italian one.

Jason, unimpressed by mere masterpieces, had settled for the living tableau on the floor beneath us, relishing the opportunity to look down on people for a change, to escape the bondage of diminutive size. Leaning my elbows on the rails I watched for a time, idly observing the antics of those mice who'd been lured from the grey skirting board of pragmatism to nibble at the cultural cheeses on offer. To'n fro they scurried. The children's activity was especially frenetic; in fact, from this height they looked as if they were performing some kind of courting ritual. Randy wee buggers, they probably thought that 'carbon dating' was some-thing new on the nookie front. Later, while wandering a corridor, I was to see a young girl fingering a man's penis. The man in question was made of bronze, and, judging by the lustre of his prong, was well used to such frontal assaults. The groperette and her giggling pals made off amid hoots of laughter.

from *Swing Hammer Swing!*, Jeff Torrington, 1992

152

GOVAN CROSS
IBROX
CESSNOCK
KINNING PARK
SHIELDS ROAD
WEST STREET
BRIDGE STREET
ST ENOCH
BUCHANAN STREET
COWCADDENS
ST GEORGE'S CROSS
KELVINBRIDGE
HILLHEAD
KELVIN HALL

PARTICK

For: Bus and Rail Interchange: Partick Burgh Hall:
West of Scotland Cricket Club.

THIS STATION was opened as Merkland Street (although often referred to as Partick West) and so remained until the time of the modern refurbishment of the system, when the opportunity was taken to move the location of the BR Partick Station to provide a joint BR/Underground interchange station.

This was the only station which suffered damage during the last war, partly due to the fact that the whole tunnel system is relatively shallow – perhaps one of the reasons why none of the tunnels were used as civilian shelters. On 18 September 1940 a bomb, probably intended for the nearby docks, landed on a neighbouring bowling green. However, both tunnels were badly breached south of Merkland Street Station, where they begin a 1 in 20 descent under the river, and the system was not fully repaired for over four months.

One story is recorded from cable days of a train which was overloaded with aggressive football fans and which failed to climb the up-gradient between Govan and Merkland Street. The fans, including fifteen who had infiltrated the driver's cabin, became more and more threatening until the driver persuaded them to get out and walk up the track to the station while he picked up the cable again and the empty train followed them to the platform.

To the SW of Kelvinside is the burgh of Partick, extending towards the Clyde. It is large enough and populous enough to outrival many a provincial town that plumes itself on its importance. The part towards the river is occupied by densely-populated streets, the denizens of which are somewhat noted for their rough character; but on the rising-ground to the N are immense numbers of detached or semi-detached villas, which render this district one of the prettiest and pleasantest about Glasgow.

from *Groome's Ordnance Gazetteer, 1893-95*

Partick was part of the Parish of Govan, on the south bank of the river, and was not annexed to Glasgow until 1912. In the nineteenth century, cotton bleaching and printing were the staple industries, but, like Govan, proximity to the river ensured that shipbuilding and marine engineering became dominant. Partick was also an important stopping point for all manner of river traffic.

Luggage apart, it would have been an awkward business to change from train to steamer at Greenock, and the usual method for families like ours was to 'sail all the way', either from the Broomielaw or from Partick Pier, the latter being for us the more convenient point of embarkation. So thither on a fine Friday, about noon, we were rattled over the stony streets in a couple of cabs.

Our ultimate destination was a farmhouse at Carrick Castle, on Loch Goil. My mother had had no opportunity of viewing it in advance, but the place had been warmly recommended to my father by a friend, as one unspoiled by man – or words to that effect.

We arrived at Partick Pier far too early. The sun shone hotly; the tide was low; it was before the days of the Clyde's purification. Not to be squeamish about it, the Clyde at Glasgow was then a big sewer. We and other families waited and waited.

In the heat babies began to 'girn'; small children grew peevish; little girls complained or looked pathetically patient. For boys there was always the entertainment of the shipping - liners, channel and river steamers, cargo vessels, barques, barquentines, brigs and schooners, dredgers, hoppers, ferries.

At last the white funnelled *Benmore* came chunking cannily down the river, already with a fair complement of passengers, for it was the first of the month. She was almost new, the first river steamer to have a 'half-deck' saloon. For some forty years thereafter she led a steady, useful existence, once distinguishing herself – about 1912, I think – by striking, one foggy morning, a sunken rock off Innellan, and lying there for a week or so, submerged to her bridge.

She came alongside; the families were shepherded on board, to find seats where they could, and the luggage was added to the existing mountains. Luggage went free then. Years later, I witnessed the indignation of a family at being charged a trifle for their piano's conveyance. The *Benmore* resumed her journey, still cannily, for every now and then appeared on the banks boards bearing the words 'Dead Slow', the warning necessary in order that the wash from steamers should break lightly against the shores of the shipyards or the dredgers at work.

And now the warm air was full of the clangour of shipbuilding. Skeleton frameworks, one after another, and hulls nearing completion rose high above the banks. One could see the riveters, like pygmies, perched aloft, and the glimmer of their fires. 'What an awful noise,' said the ladies, while the men complacently surveyed the tremendous scene of industry – and prosperity. What would not all of us give to hear that hammering again? How merry to our ears it would sound today!

On the other side of the river we called at Govan – where the *Orient*, of the line of that name, almost completed, lay moored, testing her propeller, churning the murky water into brownish foam – and Renfrew, where another family or two joined us.

from *I Remember*, J J BELL, 1932

Rather like Kinning Park, on the opposite bank of the Clyde, Partick's small riverside streets were crammed with marine repair yards, engineering workshops, foundries and chandlers' stores.

Amongst the leading industries of which Partick forms an important centre must be classed that of the various branches of brass-working represented by the old-established house of Mr Archibald Low, trading under the style of the Partick Brass Foundry Company.

The business was founded about half a century ago and has since been greatly developed by the well-directed energy and enterprise of the successive proprietors of the undertaking. The premises comprising the foundry are situated at 78 Merkland Street, and include a spacious showroom having a frontage of 60 feet in which is displayed the large and comprehensive stock of baths, water closets, and other sanitary appliances, combining all the most recent improvements and every description of plumbing and gas-fitting requisites, &c. Adjoining the showroom are the plumbers' workshops, and here also are situated the offices. In the rear, approached by gateway entrance, is the brass foundry, comprising spacious accommodation for the various departments and fitted throughout with plant and machinery of the best type. The trade done by the firm is principally in connection with ships' plumbing and sanitary work generally, but also includes house plumbing and gas fitting and every description of brass founding.

from an advertisement in *Strattens' Glasgow and its Environs*, 1891

Had Charles Duff, unemployable painter and ex-corporal of the Highland Light Infantry during the 14-18 World War, raised his head as he passed from the close-mouth to Mr Tim O'Rafferty's Five Shamrock Bar, he would have seen a remarkable twelve feet of sunset between the gable walls of two tenement blocks. But as Duff was not in the habit of raising his head except when in the act of lowering a drink, this effect was denied him. And for Duff, as for three-quarters of a million others, the bloody garments of the dying sun did not exist.

Perhaps the most magnificent and most characteristic setting was provided by the Dumbarton Road at Partick. Here, barred by a railway bridge, across which ran a gargantuan advertisement for an Irish firm's stout, the effect was such that it attracted the attention of a Highland policeman. The policeman, who had been born and brought up in the Isle of Skye, had little use for the more noteworthy and spectacular of Nature's effects. But for a brief moment he was impressed.

This Gael in uniform, meeting the sergeant at the foot of Crow Road, remarked in a casual tone that the sun was very red tonight, whatever. The sergeant, also a Gael but from the Stoer district of Sutherlandshire, did not give himself as much trouble as look, but inquired rather peevishly if the constable had managed to collect his winnings on the 3.30. When the constable informed him that there had only been five runners, the sergeant swore as vividly and luridly as the western sky was, at the moment, coloured.

from *Major Operation*, James Barke, 1936

Before Partick began to experience the refurbishment of recent years, there was, as elsewhere, a period of semi-dereliction following the heyday of the shipbuilding and maritime industries.

A mean wind wanders through the backcourt trash.
Hackles on puddles rise, old mattresses
puff briefly and subside. Play-fortresses
of brick and bric-a-brac spill out some ash.
Four storeys have no windows left to smash,
but in the fifth a chipped sill buttresses
mother and daughter the last mistresses
of that black block condemned to stand, not crash.
Around them the cracks deepen, the rats crawl.
The kettle whimpers on a crazy hob.
Roses of mould grow from ceiling to wall.
The man lies late since he has lost his job,
smokes on one elbow, letting his coughs fall
thinly into an air too poor to rob.

A shilpit dog fucks grimly by the close.
Late shadows lengthen slowly, slogans fade.
The YY PARTICK TOI grins from its shade

156

like the last strains of some lost *libera nos*
a malo. No deliverer ever rose
from these stone tombs to get the hell they made
unmade. The same weans never make the grade.
The same grey street sends back the ball it throws.
Under the darkness of a twisted pram
a cat's eyes glitter. Glittering stars press
between the silent chimney-cowls and cram
the higher spaces with their SOS.
Don't shine a torch on the ragwoman's dram.
Coats keep the evil cold out less and less.

from *Glasgow Sonnets*, Edwin Morgan, 1972

Partick is still a thriving, distinctive place, and has always been one of those areas which people pass through on the way to or from other places – a staging-post.

Apart from occasional week-end trips with my mother, longer visits to one or other of my relatives' farms, and the annual summer holiday, my favourite excursion was one which I enjoyed almost every Saturday afternoon for a year or two, with my grandparents. Although there were three or four picture-houses in Paisley which gave afternoon performances, they remained faithful, for some reason, to one in Partick – a district of Glasgow on the north bank of the Clyde in which they had lived before coming to Renfrew. Perhaps they simply enjoyed returning to a neighbourhood for which they still had great affection; perhaps they thought it more of a treat for me than simply going to Paisley, a straightforward journey to a town which, whatever its worthiness, lacked the glamour of Glasgow . . .

There were two ways in which we could go to the picture-house in Partick and it was an agonising business to choose which it was to be. We could go by tramcar to the Ferry, cross the Clyde in the chain-bound tub whose vertical engine could be studied during the voyage, and on the northern bank take another tramcar straight to Partick. Or we could get off at Renfrew Cross and change into a tram that went eastward through the flat fields to Govan Cross where we would go down into the cable-drawn subway train and be carried under the Clyde to Partick. Both were journeys of much complexity and infinite variety, and no repetition could stale my intense enjoyment.

from *Scotland the Brave*, Iain Hamilton, 1957

Traffic on the river has all but ceased, and the chain-ferries and the trams have gone, but the Subway goes from strength to strength, carrying about fifteen million passengers a year. In recent years there has been examination of schemes to extend the Subway – a northern extension

from Kelvinbridge to Summerston via Kirklee; a western extension from Govan to Glasgow Airport; and an eastern loop from Bridge Street out to the East End and back to Cowcaddens. Cost factors have ruled out any such plans for the foreseeable future, but the system as it exists has a secure future. However, in the summer of 1996, proposals for a modern £170 million tramway system received a terminal setback when a Parliamentary Commission refused consent for development, without having to give reasons or justify its decision.

The present-day 'toy train set' would probably confound many of those who brought it into being a hundred years ago.

Glaswegians have always been sensitive to the peculiarities of this tiny railway system. It would be pleasing to feel that, as the modern Clockwork Orange whisks them through the original 11ft diameter tunnels, they are equally sensitive to that 'sense of place' which this volume has had in focus.

With luck, Glasgow's new Subwayfarers will pause briefly from the football pages to appreciate something of the journey they are making, the places they are passing, and the writers who have conjured such a wealth of images of their city.

BIBLIOGRAPHY

Apart from those books referred to in the text, there are many other sources of information about the city of Glasgow and its literature. Those listed below constitute a small selection with relevance to this volume:

Clyde Navigation by John F Riddell, John Donald, 1979

Early Travellers in Scotland edited by P Hume Brown, first published in 1891, and reprinted by James Thin in 1978

Glasgow in 1901 by 'JH Muir', Hodge & Co., 1901

A Glasgow Collection, Essays in honour of Joe Fisher edited by Kevin McCarra and Hamish Whyte, Glasgow City Libraries, 1900

Glasgow Diary by Donald Saunders, Mainly, Polygon, 1984

Glasgow and its Environs by 'Senex' (Robert Reid), published by Robertson, Glasgow, 1884

The Glasgow Novel, a Survey and Bibliography by Moira Burgess, Scottish Library Association/Glasgow District Libraries, 1986

Glasgow Observed edited by Simon Berry and Hamish Whyte, John Donald, 1987

Glasgow Streets and Places by James Muir, CA, Wm Hodge & Co, 1899

The Glasgow District Subway, its construction and equipment printed anonymously in 1905

The Glasgow Subway by DL Thomson and DE Sinclair, 1964

The Glasgow Subway by Paul Kelly and MJ Willsher, published by the Light Railway Transport League, 1978

Groome's Ordnance Gazetteer, 1893–95

History of the Glasgow and South Western Railway by Wm McIlwraith, published by John Tweed, Glasgow, 1880

I Belong to Glasgow by Gordon Casely and Bill Hamilton, Nexus Press, 1975

Industrial Archaeology of Glasgow by John R. Hume, Blackie, 1974

In the Kibble Palace by Stewart Conn, Bloodaxe Books, 1987

Kirkwood's Dictionary of Glasgow and Vicinity published by John Menzies, 1884

Mungo's Tongues edited by Hamish Whyte, Mainstream, 1993

Noise and Smoky Breath an illustrated anthology of Glasgow poems, 1900–1983, edited by Hamish Whyte, Glasgow Libraries, 1983

The Origin and History of Glasgow Streets by Hugh Macintosh, 1902

People's Palaces, Victorian and Edwardian Pubs of Scotland by Rudolph Kenna and Anthony Mooney, Paul Harris, 1983

The Second City by CA Oakley, Blackie, 1967

The Statistical Account, Vol. XIV, 1798

Strattens' Glasgow and its Environs, 1891

Streets of Stone edited by Moira Burgess and Hamish Whyte, Salamander Press, 1985

Workers City, edited by Farquhar McLay, published by Clydeside Press, 1988